Parenting Children:

LEARN HOW TO BE A LOVING AND EFFECTIVE PARENT

Jennifer Garden

© 2017

COPYRIGHT

Parenting Children: Learn How to be a Loving and Effective Parent

By Jennifer Garden

Copyright @2017 By Jennifer Garden

TABLE OF CONTENTS

INTRODUCTION: A TIME OF

TREMORS

This book is written from the viewpoint of the father, as he relives his experiences raising his child. In many ways, he is the ideal, although imperfect, parent. He doesn't exist, as you would suspect, but the stories in here about parental and childhood experiences are based on *real-life*.

Within these chapters, there are typical dialogues experienced parents have had with their children. The dialogues are also based on real-life occurrences. You can easily adapt these interactions to suit your own circumstances. Practical tips will be presented that you can apply to your situation. The dialogues within are amusing at times because your beautiful children possess a refreshing outlook on life the rest of us have long since outgrown. Children tend to get chronic cases of the "giggles," and you will giggle too as you witness your children assigning childlike interpretations of a word you have uttered. Because of this book, you will have a very rare chance to peek at our world through the mind of a child.

There are also stories herein that portray real-life successful and unsuccessful experiences others have experienced. Sometimes it helps to know what-not-to-do.

Topics included:

- Bullying
- Dealing with an Attention-Deficit Hyperactive Disorder (ADHD) or other learning difficulty
- Teaching children an awareness of their feelings
- Helping children learn to control their emotions
- Teaching children empathy and respect for another's feelings
- Peer pressure
- The Internet and cyber bullying
- Sensible and effective discipline
- Handling social interaction

This book is energized by solid psychological and biochemical facts one should know in order to take on the awesome and laudable challenge of effective child-rearing.

Raising a child is one of the most challenging tasks you face in life. It is a daunting and selfless pursuit of the highest order. Nonetheless, raising children is one of the most rewarding experiences you will ever have. You already know that you not emerge from that experience unscathed, but you will find within you the courage of a superhero, despite your misgivings.

Raising a child for the first time is like mounting a complex child car seat without an instruction booklet. It's your responsibility not to be perfect, just to get your child and yourself through the day and be alive and happy at the day's end. The trophy you deserve for doing that is invisible. Your trophy and your reward is *Love – pure, powerful, and everlasting.*

CHAPTER 1: NATURE AND NURTURE

There he was! So tiny, so delicate! Your world paused in time, and you were enveloped in wonder and awe. How is it possible for anyone that small to become your size one day? All babies do – somehow. Then you looked upon your little wonder lying there, flailing his arms and legs. Wow! He can't do anything! That's when the parental fear strikes. It is all up to you and your spouse. Everything! Shouldn't your child have some milk now? "No," said Mom. "He wants to sleep."That's when you realized he wasn't entirely impotent.

You looked at him and wondered who he will look like. Mom or Dad? As you analyzed him, you silently admitted to yourself that he doesn't look like anyone you know! A tiny little head with just a hint of hair. A nose that looks like the baby nose seen in photographs worldwide. Nevertheless, you commented that he looks like your wife, and she said he looks like you. This is the first of many concessions you made in the years to come.

Perhaps you have other children, and you turn to his sister, Emma, as she marched in the room and gave her baby brother a prolonged and critical stare. "His eyes aren't even open!" she exclaimed.

"No, not yet," you explained. "It will take a while."

"How long? When is he going to be able to play with me? You said I would have a new playmate!"

You then took her into her room and explained the facts to her. You told her ways in which she can help with the raising of her brother. Then you reassured her that you will inform her right away when her baby brother's eyes will open. You handed her a little stuffed animal and told her to place it in his crib. She seemed pleased about that.

That was the beginning of a long list of loving negotiations you need to make between siblings. This tiny package you are gifted with comes along with a huge list of requirements.

In the beginning, you patrolled the hallway like a dutiful sentry. One day, the baby let out an ear-splitting cry. Your daughter who was peeking into his room raced away. You were amazed that two little baby lungs smaller than your fists could render such a sound. Who needs that baby monitor we have when the whole house reverberates with his cries?

Mom arrived swiftly, picked him up, and remarked that he will be in your room for just a short time, but the monitor will be useful when he's in the nursery or when she is downstairs.

Survival of the Body – First Things First

Then Mom caressed the baby and sat in the rocker. "He's hungry," she said, and breast-fed him. As she rocked, she explained that the rocking will imitate the movement he felt when he was in the womb.

"How do you know these things? Maybe he was hurting somewhere," you replied, as your protective paternal role emerged.

"A mother just knows. You will too. Remember the mouse in the garage?"

You reflected back to that Saturday afternoon when you and your wife were cleaning out the back garage. When you removed a large piece of cardboard near the work shelves, Mother Mouse scampered under an old blanket with her little pink babies still hanging on to her nipples. One poor little one lost his hold. He squirmed and squeaked in desperation. Then your wife picked him up every so gently and placed his little mouth back on the nipple. She forbade you to get rid of the mouse and her tiny babies. Your back garage was then used to store your classic car, to use for your workshop, and run a mouse house. For generations to come, no doubt. The maternal instinct permeates most warm-blooded species, and even a few cold-blooded species as well. This should all come natural to you, but you're not sure you can trust yourself.

Mom finished feeding your little boy and she proceeded with "burping" him. She supported his head and held him up to her shoulder where she had a little towel, and tapped him gently on the back to let him dispel any air in his tummy. Whimsically, you remembered your own "burping sessions" in the third grade when you and the other boys would all burb just to see who could burb the loudest.

After he let out a few satisfying burps, you pondered to yourself *"Why do they need to do this? Why aren't they fully functional yet? Surely, he's not defective."* You certainly weren't trained in baby biology, but somehow you sensed what his basic survival needs are. Instinct began to kick in.

Mom put him back in the crib, and he fell asleep. Then the two of you tip-toed out of the room.

Parenting is a tremendous responsibility and all parents merit applause for making all efforts to provide for their baby's needs. Babies need around 16 - 25 ounces of milk per day from the age of 1 month to six months. Larger babies may need slightly more. All parents need to consult a pediatrician to assess a baby's needs through the early developmental stages. However, in some isolated instances, your baby knows best! Consider Timmy's story.

Timmy First Picnic

When little Timmy was five months old, his mother asked the pediatrician if it was time to start him on solid food. The pediatrician indicated it was still a bit too early.

One evening, Mom and Dad had Timmy perched up in his high chair on their deck while they were serving themselves barbequed ribs. Mom placed her food-filled plate on a tall table while she grabbed the barbeque sauce. After she turned back, one of her ribs had been taken off her plate. She glanced over to Timmy who was supposed to be drinking a little bottle of expressed milk. Timmy sat up there – proud and happy. The milk bottle was rolled into the corner of his tray, while he gnawed enthusiastically on Mommy's pilfered barbequed rib! Sometimes babies know best.

The Trial and Error Method of Parental Learning

One evening, a blood-curdling cry came from the baby's crib. The alarum had brashly sounded. The baby book came out, and you perused it while running into the room. Not hunger…Mom felt his diaper, and started removing it. Wow! What a stench it was! It was no longer the academic exercise that you reviewed in the book. Then you remembered his sister, Emma, and invited her in to watch you put on his diaper. You knew you must both be careful of the jealousy factor. She watched with great interest as Mom tenderly washed your little boy, dried him off and placed him on the changing table. It was your turn next. As you bent over to powder him, you got shot in the face with urine! Little Emma, although astonished, laughed heartedly. Then you dried your baby and practiced the diaper change. Oh, yes, you remembered now from your experiences with Emma who would always fuss and wiggle. Your boy was no different. Perhaps he will run track someday.

Survival of the Self

1. Basic Psychological Needs

Yet another cry pierced the quiet from your baby's crib in the early evening one day. You knew he was fed in the middle of the night, and again at daybreak. His diaper was changed. You ran into the room. What could be wrong now? Mom was already there, picked him up, and rocked him in her arms. Like magic, it worked. That's when you reminded yourself that you've been micromanaging his development by focusing almost exclusively upon his biological needs. According to Engle & Lhotska, "Care refers to the behaviors and practices of caregivers (mothers, siblings, fathers and child care providers) to provide the food, health care, *stimulation and emotional support* necessary for children's healthy survival, growth and development."

Mabel and Baby Mike

A few years ago in the waiting room at a clinical psychologist's office, his psychological assistant noted that a woman by the name of Mabel had her baby in his carriage next to her. Every time the baby fussed or cried, Mabel leaped up and put a bottle into his mouth. There were no plush animals in the carriage and there were no hanging colorful beads dangling from its hood. The child was simply staring at the white ceiling overhead. He

> *appeared to be fatter than most children his size and age,*
> *carrying far more weight than baby fat would account*
> *for. The assistant made mention of this to the doctor*
> *after Mabel entered the room for her session, so he could*
> *address the issue.*

Sometimes the obligations of parenting responsibly lie heavily upon the parents and there can be a strong need on the part of the parents to ease the burden. You already know how much breast milk or formula your child should drink as a baby. Whole milk may cause some weight gain because of the fats in it. Nevertheless, those fats are wholesome within moderation. Too much milk, on the other hand, may cause a psychological dependency as well as physical health consequences. Milk is not a pacifier. In Mabel's case cited above, it may have been used as something to keep the baby quiet. Mabel may unwittingly be sentencing herself to a number of years of "pacifying" her child by teaching him that Mom will take care of it whenever her child wants something. That can cost a small fortune in a toy store.

Sometimes eating carries the illusion of comfort when one is distressed or depressed. In its extreme, a dependent personality may result by fostering an atmosphere in which much gratification is obtained from food or even friends. We all know such people as adults. They are the ones who find decision-making difficult without consulting a "committee of friends," from whom they get advice and emotional support for nearly everything they say or do.

According to Cline and Fay, excessive loving can also stunt a child's confidence. They said, "We want to do everything humanly possible for our children so that someday they can strut confidently into the real world. And we do it all in the name of love. But love can get us in trouble – not love itself per se, but how we show it. Our noblest intentions are often our own worst enemy."

2. Need for Love and a Sense of Belonging

Abraham Maslow, the world-famous psychologist from the 20th century, delineated a hierarchy of needs for all humans. They are innate and persist throughout life. As your children grow, these needs will become more sophisticated. Nonetheless, they start immediately upon birth. On the second rank of his hierarchy sits the need for love and belongingness. You remembered the time when Mom held your little baby in her arms to comfort him. He needed reassurance he was loved. He needed to know she is the Mom and you are the Dad. In fact, he seemed to have an "emergency need" to know that she and you love him and he loves you in return. He wants to be soothed by the understanding that you belong to him, and he belongs to you.

Malik's Crisis

One day when a mother was grocery shopping, she very vigilantly held little Malik's hand. Occasionally, she would draw it away to use two hands to examine a product on the shelf. As she moved forward inspecting some of boxes, a little girl slipped in to look at an adjacent shelf. After Malik's mother had chosen a product and dropped it into her cart, she reached down with her hand. The little girl nearby put her own hand into Malik's Mom's hand, and she moved forward.

> *Suddenly, a very loud voice emerged from a very small boy a yard behind her, "HEY, MOM! YOU TOOK THE WRONG KID!" Shoppers from two aisles heard it, and two mothers with two red faces resolved the problem post-haste. The need for love and belongingness arises quite early and persists throughout life.*

As the clock of time inevitably raced ahead, your child faced the first day at school. Mom was ushered to the front hallway of the school while your little boy was taken to his classroom. She stood there in fear and trepidation along with all the others undergoing the same ordeal. All eyebrows were raised in anxiety as everyone watched their children disappearing around the corner at the end of the hall. She and a few others peered into the classroom window trying to get a glimpse of their children. After the principal scooted them away, the mournful crowd returned to the nest *sans* one child. You called her from the office. "How was it?" you asked.

"Horrible! Our little boy has left home!"

You both know that hurdle isn't going to visit for a while yet, and reassured her. But she can't be comforted so easily. When you got home, you reminded her that your older child, Emma, fared quite well. The house was in chaos that day, Mom was upset, but your little boy was quietly coloring at the kitchen table. "So how was school?" you asked.

"I'm never going back there again! I had to nap in front of all the other kids. They were all doing stuff!"

Uh...oh. Perhaps you both overdid it with affection. You can appeal to children's logic by telling little stories to help them adapt. So you elicit more information about your boy's first day. He admits that he had fun with the toys and sorting things. Next, it's story time for you and your child. Maybe you tell a story about the baby birds who grew too big for the nest, and wouldn't leave it. So, they never learned how to fly or how to have fun in the trees. In time, you want your child to tell you real-life stories about his experiences, worries, and concerns.

Both of you want to open a dialogue with your child, being careful to encourage openness. Of course, you don't want to impose rigidity upon him, and mimic a drill sergeant. Perhaps your dad was like that, and you feel that only the more valuable principles your parents taught should be preserved.

When children enter middle school, become pre-teens, and assume all the dimensions of those stormy teenage years, you want them to feel comfortable sharing their experiences. You want them to ask for advice. They won't always do that, but both of you keep your fingers crossed knowing there will be mistakes.

3. Esteem Needs

Self-esteem and the esteem of others is the bulkhead of psychological survival and a key for success and happiness. It is especially important during the child's preteen and teenage years. We all remember the roller coaster of our own years when acceptance by the peers becomes overwhelming. You know the early symptoms experientially. Then it happened unexpectedly and is very much unwelcome.

It was Thursday, you recall, when your cell phone rang as you drove home. It was your wife. You knew she would never call you while driving, unless there's a crisis. Your blood pressure rose as you answer.

"He's not home yet! Football practice is over. I called the school, and he left an hour ago. Bert was going to drive him home, but Bert said Brian told him he had to meet me at the store. That wasn't true."

"Did you call the other parents we know?" Of course she had, but you're at a loss. Sometimes parents feel they must have solutions to allay the fears of their spouse.

You called the police and the nearby hospital when you got home, while your wife tooled around in the kitchen distracting herself with dinner preparation. The hospital had no emergency admissions under your son's name. The police – as expected – indicated that a missing person report cannot be filed until 24 hours have passed. The police then hint that perhaps he ran away. You're insulted because you know Brian, and he wouldn't do that...you didn't think. There was nothing else to do about it, so you fell back on the comforting family routine – supper. Besides, your daughter needed to eat. She was on some kind of crazy diet and the two of you had to coax her to consume some protein. At the table, you told her about your dilemma, and she was concerned.

The front door opened. Brian strutted in, plunked his books on the couch and entered the kitchen. All three of you looked at him and lapsed into silence. *Gasp!* The hair on top of his head was dyed blonde!

"Where were you? What happened to your hair?" Secretly you wanted to bellow at him, but glanced at his sister. Then the two of you left the table to have a private discussion with your son. His sister tried desperately to eavesdrop of course.

"You know the rules, Brian. If you're delayed, you're supposed to call us."

"Yeah, but I forgot the time." That's when you wanted to shake the daylights out of him. However, you remembered your own dad who was so quick to lay down the law. So you know that dialogue is the better alternative.

"Whatever came over you to dye your hair?" your wife asked in desperation.

"All the kids are doing it." *'All?'* you thought to yourself.

That's when you fell back on the original dialectical approach you and your wife agreed to, and used with him since he was very young. You expressed your love for him and told him that you care about him. If he isn't home, you share with him the fact that his failure to ask or inform you awakens your feelings as well. Your wife exhorted him, "Please don't do that to us again." He seemed surprised that his behavior had such an effect on his family. Elicit thoughts and feelings from your child regarding lying, and carefully lead him into applying some common sense guidelines to decision-making. As for consequences, it is recommended that you give him a choice. After that incident, he decided he would stay at home for a few Saturdays and help around the house. Naturally, there were "pout sessions" on the first Saturday. He sat in his room doing nothing, hoping you'll check on him. But you didn't. Emotions are short-lived, and he will come out of his self-imposed confinement when he's bored. You had now set up a win-win situation. You win because he started helping you in the garage. He wins because he rejected being led by his feelings. His thoughts guided him instead.

Esteem needs are part of being human. Humans are social beings. Most animals are, with some rare exceptions. The polar bear hunts alone, but spends his life in a cold world.

Teens are particularly vulnerable because they are still formulating their adult personality. They can be prone to depression and feelings of alienation if they think others "don't like" them. What's worse is the fact that they lose focus on their future. They shrink their environments to the here-and-now, giving little thought to that someday there will be no classmates to pass judgment. Then you recall the last class reunion. That's when you discovered that the guy voted "Most likely to succeed" didn't.

4. Security in Structure

Routine can be a drag. However, we all depend upon it in order to progress. It is a necessary compromise with our environment. If you are graced with the opportunity to spend some workdays doing your job from home, what happens on the first day or two? Yes, you stay in your pajamas until noon. The afternoon is spent eating and puttering around. By the evening, reality strikes. That day you got all of nothing done! You are shaken out of your shoes, and feel lost and insecure. That dreadful routinized structure is gone. In fact, your child feels that way too if structure is lacking.

When your son came home from school on his first day in junior high school, you remember that he looked frantic.

"So how did it go?" you asked at the time.

"I got into trouble for wandering the hall! We have to change classrooms now for different subjects. That's stupid," he complained loudly. "Then all the kids opened their lockers to change books. *Bang! Bang! Bang!* I had trouble finding mine in the bedlam." You smiled, as you recall that even your teachers used to rush out of the classrooms right before the buzzer went off and pandemonium erupted in the hallway. So you shared your story with him and sympathize. You know that it is an adjustment, but another structure will replace it. Structure grants a sense of security.

Sometimes children are deprived of structure. Below is the story of "Sneaks" – the street name of one young man who grew up in a poverty-stricken area in the inner-city.

"Sneaks"

Almost every day Sneaks walked the streets. He lived with his mother, but never knew his father. Sometimes his mother was home; sometimes she wasn't. Sometimes there was food in the refrigerator; sometimes there wasn't. So he went garbage-picking. Occasionally, Sneaks would do some shoplifting. He attended school infrequently and only when his mother came home and insisted upon it. The school tried to contact the home to no avail and alerted the juvenile division. Sneaks was clever and learned all the rules of streets. By the age of 15, he was still set in a physical

---

> *survival mode. It wasn't until he absconded with a motorbike that the authorities sent him to a juvenile facility. He was belligerent while there and hollered a great deal. Despite his daily complaints about having "to go through all these changes," he came to rely upon the structure and schedule he claimed to detest. It was far better than survival of the fittest. Sneaks was a small boy, but he learned to compensate by the use of his intelligence. Sneaks lived by his wits alone.*

Security also exists in discipline. Although punishments and penalties are unpleasant for your child, at least he knows what to expect if he misbehaves.

One evening, your son arrived home in time for supper as usual. After supper, the doorbell rang.

"Hi, you don't know me. I'm Ben Mackin from Clinton Road."

"I'm Peter Holland. Nice to meet you."

Ben then continued. "My son and his friends have a clubhouse in an empty lot near our house. Your boy opened the padlock and broke in. The place is a mess, and the lock is missing."

"My son?" you asked. Then, as you turned around, you noticed that your boy was hiding behind a living room chair. *"Am I raising a safecracker or a locksmith?"* you wondered to yourself.

"Brian, come here!" Timidly, he came forward. "Did you do that?"

Even more timidly, he nodded his head. "Yes," he mumbled.

"Apologize to Mr. Mackin, and we're going to go to Clinton Street to apologize to his son…his friends, too, if they're available."

Then your son apologized to Ben, and you tell Brian, "Now, give Mr. Mackin the padlock."

"It's not here," Brian responded. "It's right near the clubhouse."

"Let's go get it."

"I need a shovel," your son said.

"A *SHOVEL?*" you asked in astonishment.

"I buried it."

Silently, you were amused. Raising children has its funny moments, even though they may not occur under ideal circumstances. After the infraction, you gave Brian a choice of penalties. He knew that was coming, but there is some security in knowing what would happen next. Cause and effect is a natural pattern, and intelligent decision-making happens when you can predict effects accurately.

[1] This procedure has since been discontinued because of unwanted side effects.

CHAPTER 2: THE WILD AND THE WILY – THE RIGHT-BRAINED CHILD AND THE LEFT-BRAINED CHILD

It is still commonly believed that a "Left-Brained" individual is dominated by his sense of logic and is more literate. On the other hand, a "Right-Brained" person was believed to be more intuitive and emotional as well. This belief is actually a myth, but it persists to this day. People started to think in these terms after Roger Sperry, David Hubel and Torsten Wiesel of the University of Chicago earned the Nobel Prize in 1981 for medicine and physiology. Their experiment had to do with a phenomenon that reduced epileptic seizures by splitting the corpus callosum. The corpus callosum is the structure in the mid-center of the brain and allows for communication between one side of the brain and the other. Once that was split, epileptic seizures were significantly reduced.[1] There were side effects,

31

however, which rocked the scientific world. One of those side effects showed that the left side of the brain controls logic and language skills, while the right side interprets and processes spatial relationships and visual comprehension. Therefore, logical thought and deductive abilities emanate from some of the area in the left-side of your brain. Creativity and skills with visualization comes somewhat from the right side of the brain. The truth of the matter is the fact that *both* sides of the brain are used in daily functioning.

Nevertheless, it is fun to believe that one side is more dominant than the other. A child who is labeled as being one who is "Left-Brained" tends to do well at math and displays organizational skills. A child who is labeled as "Right-Brained," might be thought of as being more artistic and visual. That child might recall a fact in a school book because he thinks of seeing the word itself at the head of a chapter. Hence, you may be the parent of a brilliant physicist like Marie Curie or more like Noah and Joseph McVicker who invented Play-Doh.

The admixture of the creative mind and the logical mind (The "Right and Left" brained people) is where we really dwell. Mark Zuckerberg perhaps typifies this well. His creative mind was that of an entrepreneur who used his intuition to sense the need for a site on which people could socialize and his logical mind was that of a computer programmer. When he married the creative with the logical, he conceived and developed Facebook.

1. "Coloring outside the lines" – The intuitive and creative child

One day, when Mom was preparing supper, her younger son and older daughter were underfoot. They loved her casseroles and especially the dessert she was preparing of home-baked cookies. Like little kittens, they scouted the kitchen. So, in the interest of her sanity, she scooted them both out to the dining room where they were given coloring books. Emma had chosen a picture of a squirrel, and scribbled crayon lines haphazardly throughout and outside his body. Just then, Dad, arrived home.

After the charming greeting (kids always seem to fly at Dad before Mom), they showed Dad their pictures so far. Mom then returned to the kitchen.

"That's very nice, Emma, you said. "Next time, why not try to keep your coloring inside the lines?"

Emma then quipped, "He needs an extra coat for the winter!" *What a clever and creative girl,* you think to yourself.

Tim's chosen picture was a car. Not a surprise. Ever since he was very young, he played with them. He even played with the carefully constructed models of antique automobiles you had on your shelf...until he was corrected, of course.

Luci and Her Dad's Presentation Paper

Luci's Dad was the head of a department in an engineering firm. Many evenings were spent at his desk in his home reading research or preparing for team meetings. After finishing one such task on his computer and printed out five finely crafted presentation papers for his staff meeting, he left hem on his desk and joined his wife in the living room. In the meantime, little Luci explored his desk and came across the papers. Oh, the high-quality paper was so smooth and glossy! She ran her hand across it and appreciated its texture. She then retrieved her colored felt pens, walked over to the papers, carefully turned the pages, until coming to some that were blank. Apparently, those were intended to separate the different sections of the presentation. Carefully, Luci placed her hand on one of the sheets and traced around it. Then she added many rings — four in all — embellished with gemstones. After that, she colored in the hand and all the golden rings and gemstones. She continued with the other papers as well.

There was much laughter at the team meeting the following day, as the crimson-faced department head apologized to his staff.

Upon his return home, the father asked Luci why she did that to his work. In reply, she said, "It seemed like such a waste to have empty paper! Besides, there were no pictures...just numbers and stuff!"

The father in the above story no doubt spent a few gentle words explaining to his daughter about boundaries. He indicated that he wouldn't consider raiding her toy box, and altering the look she had bestowed upon her dolls. However, little Luci of the story also taught her father something, too. After that incident, he began adding a few illustrations and the like to some of her presentations. The father can his children, but the children can likewise teach their parents.

Besides that, Luci's response to her father's inquiry as to why she drew on the blank pages can serve as an insight into the integration of the creative with the logical. A creative child may also use her logical mind as well. Within her narrow parameters of a child's environment, there is an integration of the creative with the logical. After all, to her way of thinking, Luci felt that it was illogical to have empty paper that communicated nothing. In a curious way, she was correct.

On that fateful day when Emma graduated college with an art degree, she continued to work at the clothing store where she worked while attending college. While Emma had a creative, intuitive aspect she– indeed – had the ability to be detailed and organized as well. Once endowed with her degree, she got a salary raise. However, her artistic abilities remained untapped. What's more, you were concerned that she was going to remain at that clothing store for the rest of her life. Her salary at the time was far below that of other peers who had gone on to work for art studios and the like. She was now a young adult, and one must refrain from the kind of coaxing you give to teenagers who aren't striving to achieve their full potential.

The best way to encourage creative children is to ask questions. Pulling experiences from their memories sometimes helps. One day, a possible solution occurred to you, and you brought it up in a conversation.

"Emma, remember the experiment you did for science when you were growing plants from lima beans?"

"Yes, I remember that. The beans I put into the sun and watered regularly grew. The beans I put down in the basement grew funny, didn't have any green coloring, and eventually died."

"So what about your art talent?" you asked. "It's not being cultivated properly is it? What happened to the lima beans grown in the dark?"

That was a rhetorical question, which beckoned no answer. Once something is said, it is said. After that, Emma became more pensive and related the story to her own experience. In time, she decided to take the risk of applying for jobs related to her chosen field. Eventually, she decided to apply to a frame shop, and was immediately hired. Later on, she ran a very large art supply concern, and also did much of the work for customers who wanted individually crafted frames for their precious art work.

Emma joined her sales skill with her artistic abilities. Thus the creative met the organized aspects of her unique skill set.

The so-called "Right Brain" united with the "Left Brain." That instance represented an integration of the various kinds of abilities a child has.

2. "Even toy parking lots have rules" – The logical organized child

It was on a Saturday in June, and you remembered finding your large toy tractor trailer when you were cleaning out the attic. It was still in fair condition. This you set aside to give to your son, Brian. After descending the old rickety attic stairway, you placed it on the sideboard. Brian was happily playing on the floor with his little cars.

"Can I play too?" you asked.

Half of the toy cars were lined up neatly, and Brian was retrieving more from his box of toys. "How do you play?" you asked.

"This is the parking lot, he explained. Get some cars out so we can park them." Humbly, you obeyed. Then, you placed a box van in the imaginary parking space backwards.

"No! No!" Brian complained. "They all go in this way," indicating that the front of each vehicle goes to the left. No one apparently backs in, you mused to yourself. Then you recalled the tractor trailer and presented it to him. Even though it was larger, having been built to a different scale, he seems delighted.

Your wife came in at that point, and asked that you give her a hand in the front yard, so you thanked Brian for the game and told your older daughter to keep an eye on him. After donning your dirty jeans for outside work, you wondered if your boy was going to be an accountant – stringent with particulars – or maybe just a parking lot attendant!

"Uncle Mike, Here's your Invoice!"

Mike's children were fully grown, but for a few days, his sister and brother-in-law asked if they could drop their six-year-old boy at his house while they went away for a brief outing. Mike worked at home as an entrepreneur who sold auto parts to auto restoration companies and individuals for their antique autos. When his nephew, Jason, arrived, he was full of energy. Mike tried to adapt to the sudden onslaught of activity as Jason and Mike's dog ran around Mike's basement office. Suddenly, Jason slipped and fell on the floor. "Yeowww!" he cried. Mike rushed over to assess the physical results of the all-too-predictable

---

calamity. A fairly bad scrape, covered in blood. Then there was that inevitable trip to the bathroom, accompanied by some heartfelt words of comfort. Out came the washcloth, the antiseptic, and the largest band aid you had in stock. Poor Jason was still sniffling and claimed to be in deep pain. Just how deep was a subject Mike didn't address, naturally. It was just superficial. So Mike had Jason sit by his desk. Not long afterward, Jason joined him and watched Mike at his computer. He was pelted with questions, and showed Jason how he wrote emails to prospective clients. "Oh, I write emails to Grandma all the time!" chirped Jason. Then Mike told him how they bought some auto parts which were shipped to their locations. After that, he showed his nephew a few invoices. "What's an invoice?" Jason asked. "A bill," replied Mike. Jason then indicated he had his small laptop with him that had email, a few games, and an art program on it. "Why don't you set up a make-believe company yourself?" suggested Mike. "Only don't send out any real emails. Just put 'pretend' ones in the section marked 'Drafts.' Don't add real email addresses either. Jason ran off into the corner and started plunking away on his little computer. Mike was relieved for a little peace and quiet.

Forty-five minutes later, Jason returned. Then he showed Mike his company "Jason, the Auto Hero." Mike smiled at the creative name.

"Can you print this out?" asked Jason, pointing to something on the screen. Mike obliged and hooked Jason's laptop to his own printer and printed the piece. Handing it to Uncle Mike, he proudly announced, "Uncle Mike, here's your invoice!"

Mike looked at it. The bill, done up in Jason's art program, was for the purchase of a 2013 Camaro engine priced at $ 4,400 !

So, as you were raising your own son, it is so vital to keep in mind that today's child learns early on, even in school, basic computer skills. In addition, this strengthens his ability to his logical, organized mind. As you reflect back on that toy tractor trailer you gave your son when he was about six-years-old, you recall how he used it. On the day you came inside from your joust with the weeding, you noted that your son's cars were gone. Only the tractor trailer sat in Brian's infamous parking lot.

Brian had made his way into the kitchen by then along with your daughter. You picked up the tractor-trailer. It felt like it weighed half a pound! Gingerly, you opened the back doors on it. Inside were jammed Brian's little cars, your lead paperweight and nearly all the pens on your desk! While you praised him for his ingenuity, and noted his ability to organize parts into a whole, you realized that there also needs to be a delicate discussion of boundaries — not unlike the discussion you had with his older sister not too long ago. This was your logical, organized son.

In time, Brian attended college and obtained a degree in biophysics. He had considered designed prosthetics for paralytics. However, he coupled his logical, mathematical mind with some creativity. Instead of burying himself in a laboratory or join a firm as a mechanical engineer, Brian decided to put some of his creative side to use. He secured a position as a marketer and salesman for a firm that specialized in demonstrating, servicing, leasing and selling medical equipment. The company needed someone with a degree like his who could instruct staffs and doctors in drug companies, research facilities and how to utilize the equipment, and interpret the results. You and your wife were delighted in his success.

CHAPTER 3: IN THE PLACE WHERE THE HEART MEETS THE MIND

There is often disquiet and skirmishes in everyone's brain, created by one's emotional responses. A compulsive neighbor decides to prune his bushes, mow his lawn, run the saw in his garage, tear down his shed and hire a group of fervent contractors to build a large new shed enhanced with a driveway entrance. When you go outside to relax on your patio in the summer sun, you are besieged by the roar of the electric pruner for hours, a raging lawn mower that desperately needs an upgrade, a squealing saw, or hammering, chopping, yelling, and the beep, beep of a piece of equipment being backed down to the end of his driveway. Already, the birds have taken off, and your dog barks at your back door in order to take refuge with your wife inside. Your stomach knots up, your teeth grit together, and your hands are clenched into fists. You're angry. You want to charge right over there and punch the guy in the face.

Of course you know that the neighbor has a right to do what he is doing. After explaining boundaries to your children, you want to respect boundaries yourself. It takes emotional control and thought to call upon your coping strategies. Your children are likewise bombarded by their feelings. Because they are still young and immature that responsibility for that onerous task falls on you.

1. Integration of Thought and Emotion

In the lower center of your brain lie two structures called amygdala that resemble large beans. They are the seat of the emotions. There is a term for that area of the brain that can be dubbed "the bully brain". It houses the amygdala. It is responsible for the fight-flight response. In fact, if anything is seen as a threat, most often the emotions may even bypass the thought area of the brain. For example, if a rabid dog confronts you, you will immediately run. You will do so without even thinking about it. All mammals, including the human being, have the instinctual need for survival. In the human being, survival also encompasses psychological survival. If a child is playing with a toy, and his sibling suddenly snatches it away, the child will holler or cry. A child needs to learn how to manipulate objects and apply his own little interpretations to his private game. Thus, with time, he will learn how to deal with his environment as he grows. No doubt, you have heard of Origami, the Japanese craft of fashioning animals and objects out of flat paper. This is an ancient practice that originated with the poor classes, at a time when the children had no toys. To compensate, they were taught how to make their own toys. A skillful child could fashion common items like chairs, tables, dogs, birds and people out of paper.

During the school year, you remember the time when you noticed that your son was getting bad grades in reading and English comprehension. Yet, you knew your boy could read and seemed to understand the stories. After you received his school report, you recalled approaching him.

"Brian, I noticed you haven't been doing well in your reading and English. I know you can read, so what happened?"

"The stories are *stupid!* They're *boring.* I don't **feel** like reading them, and answering all the dopey questions they ask about the stories."

Here you have a feeling entering in. Your child doesn't **feel** like doing something, so he dispenses with it. He is permitting his "bully brain" to rule his actions.

As a responsible parent, you sit down with Brian while he does his English homework. The entire session is a nightmare of haranguing and complaining. By sheer force of will and loving patience on your part you get him through his homework. However, you cannot sit next to him in class and do the same. At the end of the school year, Brian flunks the subject. Knowing he won't get promoted to the next grade without attending summer school for English.

Summer comes, and Brian bounced into the room.

"Dad, when does the computer camp you promised me start up?"

"Brian you can't go to the computer camp. You have to take classes in English."

"But you *promised!*" he hollered.

"I promised you could before you flunked English. Now you have a timing conflict. English class is help while computer camp is in session."

Oh, you remember those famous words uttered so many times: *"But you promised!"* Children think in absolutes and have yet to learn about the influences of change and the conditions that alter one's direction. Thus you pull from examples in your own life and lovingly remind him that he will not move on to the next grade level, if he doesn't complete his task.

"Now, how would you feel if all your other classmates move on to the next grade, and you have to stay behind and repeat the year with the younger kids?"

Brian stopped, thought about it, and pictured himself with the younger children.

"Yeah, I guess I have to go to summer school...but I'm going to *HATE* it!"

"It's OK to hate it, Brian, but it needs to be done."

It is absolutely essential for all parents to permit their children to have feelings. <u>However, they don't have to act on them.</u> At times in your own life when you've shared a problem with another, how many times has the other person said: "You shouldn't feel that way!" On the contrary, you have a right to have a feeling. It may be a misinterpretation from your viewpoint, but your feeling is real. No one has the right to deny you a feeling. You and you alone are the only one who may (or may not change) that feeling. It is how you handle it that truly matters. The same is true for children. They are little people.

Tina and the Table

A couple was once invited to the home of the husband's sister-in-law for a large family celebration. A cousin, his wife and child, Tina, were also invited. They had moved away far from you and everyone was looking forward to seeing them after so much time had passed. Twelve people were at the table when the dinner started. Little Tiny sat in her booster seat placed on her chair and was seated next to her mother, as she was still quite young. Everyone was enjoying each other's company immensely. As Peter, one of the brothers, glanced across from him, he noticed that Tina wasn't there. So, he nudged the hostess and whispered to her "Where's Tina?"

"Tina's under the table."

"UNDER THE TABLE?" he asked more loudly.

"Sssssh! Tina doesn't like to sit at the table, so her parents let her sit on floor under it."

"But she's not going to eat," remarked Peter.

"Oh, but she is eating. Her mother slips food down to her, and she eats it from a dish on the floor!"

"Are you telling me that they feed her like a dog?"

"Unfortunately, yes."

The child psychologists, Cline and Fay call this kind of parent "The Laissez-Faire Parent." They have said that these parents "decide to let their children raise themselves. Some have bought into the theory that children are innately born with the ability to govern themselves, if just given the time and opportunity, and will eventually grow into successful and creative people if the parent would just stay out of the way and not interfere."

All parents get frustrated when children let their emotions fly. Parents sometimes try to "bribe" their children in order to keep them well-behaved. If you bring your child to the store, but he gets restless and cranky, you will be tempted to buy her a toy in exchange for peace. "...Only if you're good," you might say. At the end of shopping trip, you march obediently into the toy section and permit her to select a toy. While that technique may be useful on occasion, imagine the day when she's twelve and wants a reward. Those rewards can get very expensive. Likewise, you certainly don't want to pay your child for doing all her chores. Servants get paid for work, but they have no filial obligations to your family. Being a member of a family is a union of love and caring mutually shared. It is its own reward, because families will help when a member is ill or needs assistance. In addition, every family member relies upon the family for friendship and companionship. Family love cannot be bought. Love is freely given. That is the nature of love.

2. Is Your Child Your Friend?

It's fun to join your children in games, isn't it? Sometimes, you may get knocked over when you join your son in a game of "touch football." As many parents have sadly learned, "touch" tends to become a "tackle" and you are thrown on the ground like a helpless heap! That's when you find out about a muscle in your right leg you never knew you had. It is healthy and fun to show your children that you, too, are vulnerable. Great respect can be derived from children who know that you are willing to demonstrate flaws as well.

There are of course the infamous boundaries to befriending your children. The pitfall is to treat them like peers. Lines of distinction between parent and child must be maintained. Some parents, oftentimes single parents, share their anxieties with their children. Take, for instance, this example:

The Bus Stop

At a clinic, a counseling intern expressed concern about one of the children she was counseling and consulted her advisor.

"Do you have a picture the child drew?" questioned the advisor. The intern then showed the advisor a picture. It showed the little five-year-old girl standing next to a sign with her mother.

The intern said that the little girl drew herself with her mother waiting at a bus stop. After examining the picture, the advisor said, "Normally, a four-year-old child isn't very much aware of bus stops and what they mean. Perhaps that child is familiar with her mother's anxiety waiting for the bus, and hoping it comes on time. Perhaps the mother may have told the child that she hoped she didn't miss the bus."

"When the little girl comes in to see me, she clings to

---

her mother. She is very insecure and nervous."

"Maybe the child is being made to share in her own mother's anxieties and feelings. That is something you might consider when you speak to the mother alone."

Negative experiences have more of a traumatic reaction upon a child than upon an adult. When a stressful event occurs, such as a car accident, children are more affected. In those situations, you may feel at a loss because you cannot adequately explain why it happened. Once, you recall having an accident with your son in the back seat. He was all right, but quite shaken.

"Why did the man hit us?" asked Brian one day. "Didn't he see us coming?"

"I don't know, Brian." Then you address his feelings and recognize them. "I guess that was scary, wasn't it?"

"Yeah! It sure was. He shouldn't have done that. Didn't he see us coming?" Here your child is expressing his feeling yet again. In this case, you will need to reassure your child that is it OK to have that feeling. Keep doing that, until your son brings up a related issue.

"Dad, why did he do that?

"I don't know, Brian. Sometimes stuff happens." You are now acquainting him with a reality of life. It is a hard lesson for a little child.

"I don't want to go out in the car again! Sometimes it's scary."

"Then you won't be able to go to school or football practice or anything like that." Here you have introduced thought into the paradigm. Upon his next car trip, he needed coaxing. After you and your son returned unscathed, he begins to learn how to neutralize his fears and supplant it with thought and logic.

Every human brain can "rewire" itself by creating new nerve synapses to compensate for psychological or physical injuries. That phenomenon is called neuro plasticity. It can be observed visually through the use of brain scans. It is the way the brain heals itself. The power of thought alone can effect change. It is how we overcome obstacles in life.

3. Name that Game!

It takes time for a child to learn the vernacular vocabulary for everyday speech. Many children are frustrated when their teachers, babysitters, and even parents don't understand what they are trying to tell you. You look upon them with love, but aren't clairvoyant. Consider this amusing example:

The "Nonuts"

When Breda was six, her parents and she sometimes

58

stopped at the ice cream vendor. Breda would listen to her parents order ice cream cones. Her father usually chose a chocolate ice cream cone, and her mother would order a "vanilla cone with no nuts." The mother usually received a vanilla cone with chocolate sprinkles on it (to substitute for the unwanted nuts). Breda always ordered the same. One time, the family went to a different ice cream place. Breda as usual ordered a "vanilla cone with no nuts." When Breda received the cone, there weren't any nuts on it, but it also didn't have chocolate sprinkles. She then complained bitterly to her parents. "Where are the nonuts? I don't have any "nonuts" on mine!" Although it took a very long time, her parents finally understood her little child lingo, and got the idea across to Breda that there was no such word as "nonuts," and chocolate sprinkles weren't "nonuts."

When someone doesn't know how to express himself, it becomes very difficult to engage with others. Humans are social and depend upon each other to learn how to build self-esteem and merit the esteem of others. Communication is an essential element in that dynamic.

According to the Center on the Social and Emotional Foundations for Early Learning of Vanderbilt University, "Young children deal with many of the same emotions adults do. Children get angry, sad, frustrated, nervous, happy or embarrassed, but they often do not have the words to talk about how they are feeling."

Children stories found in e-books, in print, and on TV can provide teaching tools you can use. Once a child has learned to identify his feeling by its correct name, the parent can lead the child to deal with the feeling by engaging thought before flying into action. You might have a child reflect upon a character in the story and teach the child words such as sad, happy, scared, and angry. Going back to the past, the father character in this book relates such an event.

One Tuesday, Brian came home as usual. He was remarkably well-behaved, went to his room and quietly started on his homework.

"He's mysteriously quiet," your wife commented. You nodded. It wasn't Brian's usual entry. Customarily, he would burst in like a tornado.

Then your cell phone rang. It was the principal.

"Brian kicked one of his classmates and knocked him down. The other boy is all right, but his teacher came to me about the incident."*Moan!* Another trip to the principal's office with our son.

"Brian!" you called to him.

He then descended the stairs and went into the kitchen to face you and your wife. "We had a call from your principal that you kicked another boy and knocked him down."

"I didn't do that!" As you looked at your son, you noticed that his eyes darted to his left. According to the experts in body language, that often means the person is lying.

In a deeper voice than normal, you said, "Look at me, Brian."

He did so, and blurted out, "But Darryl wouldn't let me play football with him and the other kids, so I got mad."

You are pleased that your son is using a "feeling word," but you need to explain the matter to him, and help him use his higher faculties to deal with the issue.

"It isn't a school rule that Darryl has to play with you, is it?"

"Well...no," he responded, looking downtrodden.

"We understand how you might feel bad about it, but there must be some other way. Does every single boy play with Darryl?"

"No. Stevie and Ian don't. Neither does Sean or some other kids."

"Have you asked them to play football or something else with you?"

"No," replied Brian. "I don't think they know how to play it well."

"Maybe you could show them...just a suggestion, of course. Or you guys might like to do something else."

Just then you saw your daughter peeking around the door eavesdropping. She had been up in her room. Children sometimes seem to have a sixth sense. You then remember the difficult time your daughter had when you moved and she was the new girl in the class. She didn't make many friends in the beginning, but learned how to compensate by spending time keeping a scrapbook full of movie stars' pictures and sayings that she printed from the Internet.

CHAPTER 4: THE CONTROL OF

FEAR

According to Renee Sorin, PhD, partnerships between parents and authority figures in school or on sports teams and the like certain kinds of fears among children are common. In the journal, *Canadian Children*, she tabulated what she observed in her studies. A summary is below:

"Fear of Separation from Attachment Figure	Fear of school/preschool
	Fear of being lost
	Fear of being alone
	Fear of being left with a baby sitter
Fear of the Unfamiliar	Fear of strange people, places and objects

	Fear of the dark
	Fear of loud noises
Fear of Being Harmed	Fear of injury accident, illness or death
	Medical fears
	Fear of deep water, fire, carnival rides and burglary
	Fear of heights
Fear of Failure, Criticism and Embarrassment	Fear of being teased
	Fear of being in a fight
	Test anxiety
	Fear of adults arguing
Fear of Insects or Animals	Fear of spiders or other insects

	Fear of snakes
	Fear of dogs, cats, bats, etc.
Fear of the Intangible	Fear of nightmares
	Fear of ghosts, monsters and omens"

1. "If this, then that..." – Dealing with Bad Memories and Superstitions

As you reflected back, you remembered a zany episode deftly performed by your wife. A bird had somehow gotten into your house, and your wife screamed. "Get him out *now!*" she beckoned to you. As you entered the living room, she was cowering in the corner and looked frantic. Your two children looked upon the scene with deep concern because Mom was so upset. Calmly, you opened the windows and pulled down the screen. Surreptitiously, you shut all the other doors to the room. Then you chased the poor creature with an upside-down straw broom until he sensed the outdoor breezes and flew out. The children were astonished, and your daughter was frightened. So you hugged your children and reassured them that everything was all right. Then you sent them out of the room.

She rested her head in her hands, and explained. "Remember when I told you my mother was superstitious? Well, she believed that a bird in the house was a bad omen. If any of them happens, then someone dies or is struck ill. I've learned to dismiss those old fears so I wouldn't pass them on to the children. I got over the fact that the foot of the bed can face the doorway, that it's OK to put your hat on your bed, that crows are innocent creatures, and there are no such beings as banshees. I just slipped up."

You smiled and put your arms around her. Unfortunately, parental fears are occasionally exposed to children.

Clearly, she overreacted and felt it important to explain her response to the children. She added that it was a foolish way to act, and quipped "Silly Mom." They giggled.

It's OK for a parent to admit to a child that she isn't always going to be a perfect parent, but will always try. After the next day, she and you reminded both children of the bird intrusion and noted that nothing bad happened.

Sometimes issues like this may need to be reinforced with your children as they get older. The attention spans of a children are proportional to their ages.

2. Fear of the Unknown and Unfamiliar

When children are about to face a new experience like a new house or a new school, their imagination never, ever is accurate. They have some level of anxiety about an unknown experience. Heck, so do you. We simply don't know what might happen in the future from beginning to end. One of difficulties that frequently arises is obsession.

Be sure to acknowledge that they have some level of anticipatory fear. Feelings are real. In addition, a child lacks the richness of environmental stimuli that you have, and may tend to think about the upcoming event often. Sometimes this even triggers a nightmare or two. There are several solutions. First of all, reassure your children. Keep them busy doing many things. Take a walk with them and explore the woods near your house. Play a few video games with them. Have your children draw pictures of what the new place or situation may look like. Encourage them to add happy elements to the pictures.

Curiosity is also a terrific substitute for fear.

Even the Deer Know

One day, a couple was walking in the woods. It was a place human beings rarely traveled. In the distance, they spotted about five deer grazing. The couple didn't disturb the deer, but watched them from time to time. The deer stopped grazing and stared at the couple. They didn't even run away. Instead, they cautiously walked around the people in very wide circles, watching and listening. After the animals left, the couple realized that those deer had probably had never seen humans before. This was a time of learning for them.

This is a nice story to tell your children. If the deer can learn new things, surely your children can too.

3. Fear of Carnival Rides

Some children are afraid of carnival rides. Many capitalize on fear with such names as: "Cliff Hanger," "Gravitron," "Ramrods," "Energy Storm," and the "Alpine." They are usually accompanied by terms like "death-defying."Human beings are often driven to experience the ultimate fearful experiences they can. The sheer intensity of heightened emotions can attract. Thus there are mountain climbers, polar explorers, and astronauts. Not only do they face their deepest fears, but they discover much about our planet and place in the universe.

The greatest cause of fear in children related to carnival rides has to do with the issue of control. In essence, these rides remove the sense of total control. One is made subject to a mechanical device. Children who refuse to take challenging rides are very often insecure in other areas of their lives.

You might recall that time when your stomach churned after going on the ride with your daughter in the twirling teacups. She loved it, and you accompanied her over and over again.

You recall saying, "Emma, Daddy's tired of the teacups." At that point, you were dizzy and imagined that your face must have turned green. *Men aren't supposed to get queasy,* you told yourself. Hastily, you ran into the men's room and let nature take its course. Mom then took over. After you reported back to the dreadful teacups, your daughter was on the ride alone, with Mom on the sidelines.

"Don't you think it's about time she tries it by herself, dear?" she asked. So, there you were – the overprotective father – subconsciously teaching your little girl that full control is needed at all times! There is a gap between the imagined and the real, and there is no totally predictable way to bridge that gap except through experience. No one can control the future. You create your future through experience.

"Emma, let's go on a different ride," you said. Her pupils enlarged and her eyebrows raised. You, Mom, and Brian wandered the amusement park until you thought your feet would quit. She expressed no interest in anything.

"Can I have some cotton candy, Mom?" she asked. Both you and she knew that was a delaying tactic.

"Maybe later, honey," Mom said. "Why not try that ride?"

"The train?"

"Yes."

"It goes up high, though. I get scared I'm going to fall."

"Look at all the kids on the train. Some are even smaller than you. And see? Some of them are laughing."

"I'll go with you, and we can hold on tight to each other." Emma froze in place.

Systematic desensitization is a long-standing practice first introduced by Joseph Wolpe in 1947. One of first steps is to have the subject breathe in very slowly and rhythmically. It is incompatible to be both anxious and relaxed simultaneously. Little by little brief exposure to the offending stimuli helps anyone control their fears – from a child to an adult. So, you tried. Emma breathed in and out slowly, but she was looking at the ground.

"Now look at the train move, and keep breathing slowly. Look! The children are getting off the train. See how they're laughing?" Emma nodded.

"Notice how the train cars are connected to the track. There's a large metal rod that wraps around a track in the center. Keep breathing slowly. Look at the wheels. They're big and strong."

Emma did so.

"Let's try it now. We'll all go," said Mom.

Carefully, Mom and Emma got into a train car, while you sat in the seat behind them.

"Dad, sit with Mom and me."

"Honey, I won't fit."

With a slight tinge of embarrassment, you got in. *Oh, the humiliations we endure to raise children,* you thought. You knew that it would look like you yourself wanted to take the ride. In fact, the ride operator looked at you curiously.

Emma held on to Mom tightly to the point Mom felt she couldn't breathe. "Just loosen up a bit," she said to Emma.

Emma maintained a rigid expression throughout the ride. Afterwards, you started a discussion relating to her feelings.

"Tell me, Emma, when were you the most scared?"

"When we got on the high section."

"You went on the high section many times. Which times were you scared the most? Think about it."

Emma paused and replied, "The first few times. Then I got used to it. Can I have some cotton candy?"

"You did very well, Emma. You were very brave. Did you at least have a little fun."

"Maybe."

"Let's get some cotton candy...you, too, Brian. You were very patient."

"I was bored until I saw that weird guy," he said, pointing to the back of a tall, heavy-set man. "He has a pony tail that swings back and forth when he walks," he said, laughing. You then remembered a teacher you had in college. He always wore a pony tail, and now he's the associate dean. *When it comes to college, perhaps it's not the clothes that make the man; it's the hair,* you thought to yourself, smiling.

The most difficult phase of desensitization is the encouragement, guidance, and even coaxing that helps a child attempt the first step. This is particular can be frustrating when children are battling with their emotions in their own mind.

In the above example, the parents rewarded their child in two ways. First, they complimented their daughter for her bravery. Then they rewarded her with cotton candy. This type of learning is called operant conditioning. When behavior is positive, children can learn that there are positive results.

You cannot keep rewarding a child with candy or food, however. Your eventual objective is to reward a child with praise and recognition. Beyond that, the reward is found in the success felt when they have conquered their fears.

4. Test Anxiety: A New Approach

If your child is unduly anxious, most literature cites relaxation exercises as a first-line defense, but may have only limited success. As a parent, you are acutely aware of the kinds of defense mechanisms your child uses most frequently. What's more, when you have solicited responses from your child related to negative issues, you have learned their thinking patterns. While fear is an intense emotion, a child has also set up a system of irrational beliefs and inappropriate coping strategies.

Children – in particular, the eldest child in the family – are more concerned when they attend school than others. In families with a smaller number of children, the eldest child (as well as the others) have less exposure to siblings and other children. Therefore, the judgmental attitudes of immature, less sensitive classmates in their classroom will impact them more acutely. At home, perhaps the older child felt like she had to be the role model for the younger child, and rightly so. In the class

Of course, most children are tense before they take a test – even those who don't show it. As adults, we are too. It relates to concerns about the future and what results of the test may mean. The results could be positive or negative. Some children become excessively anxious before tests. Yet, there are others who might act blasé about it, which is the less common reaction.Some of these might be related to:

a.   Feelings of low self-esteem

b.   Obsessive need to win and to succeed

c. Learning disabilities

Recognize that your child has anxiety about a test. Statement such as: "You shouldn't be nervous," might been apprehended by the child that they are doing something wrong. Feelings are real, and really felt. What you want to do is to help your children bypass their emotional array, and learn how to apply logic and reasoning. You want your children to reflect upon the reasons why they are overanxious about a test. By asking some gentle questions, you will discover the ill-fitting beliefs your child holds regarding the purpose and value of testing.

5. Low Self-esteem

Many children experience test anxiety, usually starting in the middle grades in school. That is the time when children become more aware of their image, and struggle with feelings of self-worth. Children from smaller families especially feel it in school because they haven't weathered through the family battles among a number of siblings.

Children sometimes have their personal images wound up with how they perform on tests. The two concepts- self-esteem and test performance are not the same. Help your child separate the two.

Many children experience test anxiety, usually starting in the middle grades in school. That is the time when children become more aware of their image, and struggle with feelings of self-worth. Children from smaller families especially feel it in school because they haven't weathered through the family battles among a number of siblings.

Exercise for Your Child:

1. *Ask her to name some adults, movie actors, or older children whom she admires.*

2. *Ask for a number of reasons why she admires that person.*

3. *Next, ask her how those people did on their ___(subject matter of the test)___ . Of course, she won't know.*

Ask your child if she admires and likes people only because they do well on tests.

4. *Ask your child if she admires and likes those people only because they do well on tests. If not, what does she admire about them?*

5. *Have your child list her positive qualities. Add some more to the list that you've observed. Remind her that those personal qualities have nothing to do with a scholastic test.*

6. Obsessive Need to Win and Succeed

Some children are extremely competitive. Normally, a willingness to compete is a laudable characteristic. However, there are some who have this all-consuming need to excel. Very often that is caused by external forces – educators' emphasis upon it, the influence of peers who traditionally perform well on exams, the external rewards like stars, certificates, plaques, or having their names announced at a graduation or other ceremonies. It is the lure of a little fame, even short-lived fame. It could also have to do with the fact that he doesn't do well in other areas of his life. (Refer to #1 above on self-esteem)

Exercise:

1. *Ask your child why he feels he must come out on top. Keep asking questions until you get to the heart of the issue.*

2. *One by one, diminish the importance of those factors. If it is external, it has nothing to do with himself as a person. It had to do with the desire to please other people or obtain some kind of certificate or plaque.*

3. *Next, ask your child where that other influential person is going to be 5 or 6 years from now. Naturally, they won't know. Or ask your child where that certificate or whatever is going to be 5 or 6 years from now. Or ask your child if anyone will remember their name even two years after it is announced from a stage or in a class. In all likelihood, the answer is "No."*

4. *Ask your child what terrible thing might happen if he*

> didn't win. The tales he will weave will sound
> disastrous.
>
> 5. Follow this with your own comments like: "Will all
>   your friends stop talking to you if you don't have a
>   perfect score?" "Will the world end if you don't come
>   out with the highest score on the test?" "Will you be
>   banished to another planet?"
>
> Be sure to recognize your child's feelings of anxiety. Share with
> him how you get anxious sometimes.

Obsession and compulsion at an early stage can affect the future of your children. In its extreme form, it can lead to an obsessive-compulsive personality disorder. Or it may lead your child to use drugs in college to stay awake throughout the night studying. Peers even make recommendations as to what drugs will help increase

Opportunities for spontaneity can be created in your family plan to dissuade a child from too much studying. Trips that cater to other interests like unplanned escapades into the woods, exploration of historical settings, museum visits, amusement parks, swimming, picnics, and the like can be introduced as weekend activities.

7   Learning Disabilities

Some children do not function well in a particular school setting for a variety of reasons. Very often, the cause is a learning disability, social maladjustment, or even a physical cause, such as poor vision or hearing. Many schools are attentive to these, and will meet with parents regarding the issue.

In the early grades, some school systems avoid the ogre of being judged by giving all the children stars on their papers, or making school activities voluntary. Reading classes in elementary school are usually separated into groups of children depending upon their abilities – the "Bluebirds," the "Robins," the "Blue Jays," and the "Sparrows," for example. Despite this neutral nomenclature, children quickly know which group excels and which one resides at the bottom. Sometimes the term the "Special" kids rears up – a term loosely given to children with minor or moderate learning disabilities who are being mainstreamed into classes. Parents most assiduously correct their children when they refer to another as one of the "Special" kids, and follow the statement with a smirk or grimace. Nonetheless, the label still is used among children. Hence, these children are stereotyped and suffer the humiliation of discrimination.

As your child grows, note the various symptoms. If he has a lot of difficulty reading, it could be a problem with visual perception. Watch how he handles a restaurant menu, and his difficulty with homework assignments. Some children see occasional words and letters backwards. That occurs within the neural networks of the brain and the processing of information from the eye or ear to the neocortex, or "thinking center" of the brain. In other words, the interpretation of sensory input gets confabulated. It is like some faulty electrical wiring in your home.

Lionel's Battle

When his younger son, Lionel, reached the stage in his

schooling when he was getting homework assignments, his father, Leroy, would guide and encourage him. That is what Leroy did with his older brother and it was quite successful. The case wasn't the same for Lionel. He took an incredibly long period of time learning some of the basic words. When he started copying some words, Leroy noticed that he was writing some of the letters backwards. After he was assigned only slightly more advanced (but easy) paragraphs, he would always become confused. Sometimes, even when Leroy read the sentences to him, they made no sense to Lionel.

The teachers discussed this issue with Leroy and his wife, and they decided to put him in a special education class. As usual, he had homework assignments of a more elementary nature. Lionel still had a lot of trouble. As result, he never did well with those either.

In time, Lionel flew into temper tantrums when his homework time came right before supper. He threw his things around the room, even breaking some of them. The boy screamed and hollered.

Leroy was totally frustrated and felt absolutely no

> *satisfaction at all.*
>
> *Further testing revealed that Lionel had dyslexia. After researching thoroughly and seeking funding, his parents located a different school that catered exclusively to dyslexic students and others with moderate to severe learning disabilities.*
>
> *At the new school, Lionel was given work that was specifically suited for him, and – for the first time – felt success at his initial tasks. His education progressed from there. In time, he was able to mainstream into regular classes again. As result of all the extra effort, parental love and patience spent on him, Lionel eventually achieved a Master's degree in Business Administration.*

Sometimes children with learning problems continue to have occasional difficulties with it. However, once they approach adulthood, they deftly develop their own coping strategies. In fact, some of the most famous fiction writers, like Stephen Cannell, were dyslexic. These children can grow up to become successful and even wealthy and famous.

8   Attention Deficit Hyperactive Disorder (ADHD)

This is a disorder often manifest in children. It interferes with learning and emotional development. Therefore, it afflicts the emotional centers as well as the higher brain activities. ADHD is characterized by:

- Lack of attention
- Impulsivity
- Hyperactivity

Unless it reaches a critical threshold, heightened motor activity by young children is normal. If your child is very active, he may or may not have ADHD, so it's important not to overreact. Consider this example of a new substitute first-grade teacher who didn't yet have her own children.

"What's That Noise?"

Mrs. Austin was under the coaching of the teacher, Mrs. Carpenter, in the next classroom. When Mrs. Austin entered the classroom, there was noise. Because they were curious about the new teacher, the children were all quiet. No one was whispering or even getting out of their seats. Yet, she heard a noise. So, she signaled to Mrs. Carpenter and asked, "What is that noise?" "It's them. They have so much pent-up energy that they squirm in their seats." "Really?" asked Mrs. Austin. "Yes, and they're good at it, too… Just wait," added Mrs. Carpenter with a knowing smile.

After a couple of hours, Mrs. Austin got accustomed to it. A short time later, there was a loud "Bang!" from the classroom, followed by laughter. Alarmed, Mrs. Austin looked around. She then spotted a small boy on the floor with his fallen chair next to him. He wore a big red face. Then he put the chair back into place, slid back into it, and looked forward. He denied being hurt and became even more embarrassed when asked. Mrs. Austin sent him to the nurse with Mrs. Carpenter, but he was perfectly all right.

> *Children are not only very active, but they seem to be made of rubber!*

There is no "sure-fire" cure for ADHD, but medication and organic treatments will help. Although it sounds contradictory, stimulant medication does help. These stimulants help in the production of the neurotransmitters dopamine and epinephrine. Both of those biochemical's serve an important role in cognition, memory, and attention. Normally, they are produced by the brain itself, but their production is inhibited in ADHD children. Fortunately, there are synthetic drugs that can be used for that purpose. Nonetheless, the child needs to be monitored for side effects and contra-indicators.

Organically, certain foods boost production of both of those substances. Bananas, avocados, dairy products, lima beans, almonds, pumpkin seeds, cheese, meat, fish, and other high protein foods will help. Dopamine is an amino acid found in many proteins.

Sugary foods should be avoided because it is released into the bloodstream quite rapidly and causes a burst of energy. Mothers are generally very well aware of that.

CHAPTER 5: THE INTERNET – A CAST OF MILLIONS

1. "Hello, World"

The blog template for WordPress applications reads just that – "Hello, World." That's the Internet. Only your guidance will help children utilize the educational and entertainment opportunities of the Internet, and avoid some of the pitfalls found in the vastness of Cyberspace. Chapter 5: Social Interaction, Bullying and Battle Fatigue

From a very early age to their teenage years, you want to encourage communication between yourself and your children. This requires a basic understanding of feelings, and the ability to name those feelings. Preschool children want you to understand their feelings, so an emotional vocabulary is an essential tool.

2. Awareness of One's Own Feelings

Typical primary words are: Happy, Angry and Sad.

Without the appropriate vocabulary, a child may act out the feeling rather than talk about it. That way, they will be enabled to verbally express their feelings and learn how to deal with them with a parent's help. Use everyday activities for examples. When his son, Brian, was three, his mother went to the store with her friends, and Brian stayed home with Dad. Tim started crying. So, you – as the father – said to him, "Mom went out to the store, and you are *sad*. You want Mom to stay home with you."

Brian nodded.

"Say it, Brian. Say 'I am sad.'"

"I am sad."

"Let's go outside and take a ride on your trike." Then you and Brian go outside. Then he hopped on his trike and scooted up and down your driveway. He is smiling.

"Riding your trike is fun. You are smiling. You are happy."

"Happy," said Brian.

Next you try to help him reflect on his feelings through memory. "Brian, when Mom went out, you were sad. Next, you rode your trike, and now you're happy. Riding your trike helps you feel better, doesn't it?"

"Yeah," he replied. "I'm happy."

Suddenly, Darby, the neighbor's door got loose and started running around Brian and his trike. Brian stopped and hollered.

"You're hollering, Brian. You're angry, aren't you?"

"I'm angry."

"What can you do about it? Keep hollering?"

"If I keep hollering, then maybe he'll run home."

"Or, maybe he won't. What else can you do about it?"

"Take him home to Mr. Cassidy." Brian then got off his trike and tried to grab Darby by his collar. The imaginative dog turned it into a game and the two of them ran around each other. It actually looked like the dog was laughing at him. Huffing and puffing, Brian stopped running. That is when Dad presented a more advanced feeling word and suggested another solution.

"You look frustrated, Brian. I think you can ask me to help you, Brian. What do you think?"

"OK, Dad."

After the two of you returned the dog to a grateful neighbor, you then took Brian inside and went to your computer with him seated next to you. After plugging in "sad children," you pulled up an image database on the internet.

"Let's look at these pictures. Those kids are sad."

Then you did the same with the other emotions.

Your daughter, Emma, then burst in the door. Immediately, she joined you and her brother at the computer.

"We're learning about feeling words, Emma," you said, hoping she would follow your lead.

"Make a sad face for Brian, Emma." Emma then pushed her nose flat and blew up her cheeks. Brian giggled loudly.

"Emma is being silly, Brian." Here you introduced a new feeling word – "silly." "Now, be serious, Emma. Sit on the carpet, and play a feeling game with your brother."

Thankfully, you were able to pop the casserole into the over, and pull out some frozen vegetables. From the living room, an occasional giggle erupted. *It's one of those rare times when there were no arguments*, you thought to yourself.

When he is older, you will want to teach your child more sophisticated words. While you may assess their general feelings through their non-verbal behavior, children feel a great relief by talking about their feelings. You want them to label their feelings more accurately, so you can open a dialogue. While "sad" may carry a certain facial expression, it is difficult to establish whether that meant "disappointed," "cranky," "worried," "bored," or the like. When he becomes a preteen and teenager, you want him to be more specific about his feelings. Introduce some of them.

Some more advanced feeling words:

Confused	Brave
Disappointed	Embarrassed
Excited	Impatient
Friendly	Proud
Ignored	Shy
Jealous	Loving
Cheerful	Bored

Surprised	Proud
Calm	Tense

3. Awareness of the Feelings of Others – Empathy Training

In order to interact successfully and be rewarded for such behavior through the esteem of others, it's essential that children understand other children feel. While a person can feel sympathy for another, it is different thing to feel empathy.

Sympathy is a sense of feeling sorry for another person. In and of itself, sympathy may not trigger an action on your part. Empathy, on the other hand, is the experience of feeling like the other feels, or imagining how another may feel in a particular situation. This is an old American Indian prayer: "Great Spirit, grant that I may not criticize my neighbor until I have walked a mile in his moccasins." Empathy induces response and can alter behavior.

In an experiment with school-aged children, they were asked to imagine how another child might feel if he was called bad names. The response was "The boy would feel bad."

Then the children were asked if they would help. Most said that they would. Why? Because every child knows what it's like to feel bad, and would want to be helped.

As his father, you remembered an event from Brian's life and used it as a real-life example.

"Brian, remember Peanuts, your teddy bear?"

"Yeah, I lost him at the hotel where we stayed."

"How did that make you feel?"

"Sad."

"I called the people at the hotel, but they couldn't find Peanuts."

"But Emma came back later and gave me a new teddy bear. I called him 'Walnuts.'"

"How did that make you feel?"

"Happy. I was happy again. He looked just like Peanuts."

"Emma once lost her doll. Do you think that helped her feel what you felt?"

Brian nodded.

Next you told Brian the story about Attean and Nathan. It is a story about a young Penobscot and a colonial boy that took place in the 17th century.

Attean and Nathan

Attean was a native American who lived in Maine. It was the middle of winter and both his parents were out looking for food. Sometimes they went out for a long time, but Attean had a warm fire in his little round house. He had a few things still to eat like berries and dried fish. One day, a little white boy was alone and outside in the cold. He had no backpack and nothing to eat. Attean knew very well what it was like to be cold and hungry. The little boy stood

---

nearby outside Attean's house and cried. He was lonely, cold and hungry. When he heard the little boy crying, he popped his head outside. Attean got scared because he had never seen a white boy before, and popped his head back inside. That boy wasn't dressed in buckskin and covered with furs like Attean was. He only had some strange dark clothes on, and had no furs. Attean thought about it, and came out again. 'That boy must be cold and hungry. I know what it's like to be cold and hungry.' So Attean signaled for the boy, Nathan, to come in. Happily, Nathan did so. Attean gave him some furs from his mom's bed and shared his food with Nathan. Later, Attean's parents came home, and helped take care of Nathan until the weather warmed. That is when Nathan learned how to make a net out of sapling shoots, and tie them together. Both boys went down by the stream and caught fish together. Soon, Attean's parents found Nathan's family who had searched the woods in vain looking for him. The two families became friends and each family learned skills from the other one.

You can elaborate on such stories to demonstrate that there are rewards for creating bonds created through empathy and mutual understanding. For example, for the above story, you can tell your child how Nathan learned how to handle a canoe, build a lean-to out of branches and pine needles, catch fish, and find berries.

4. Conflict Resolution

Brian and Emma were playing in the backyard on Saturday morning. You your wife were on the patio, enjoying a cool drink. Then the two of them headed for the tent you had erected for them. Suddenly, from within the tent comes an outcry, rapidly followed by screaming. Both ran out and up to the two of you to resolve. They were red-faced and sweaty. You both decided it was time for them to learn about conflict and develop some workable solution

While the emotions raged in their systems, their higher brains were squelched out. No point in engaging logic then. Stress impedes thinking. A real-time example:

a. Cooling Off

"Emma, go sit on the grass over there," you said, pointing to your left. "Brian, sit on the grass over here," you added, pointing to your left. "Both of you breathe slowly until you calm down."

After that, you want them to label their feelings and express their points of view one at a time.

"Now each of you is going to name their feelings – one at a time – and tell the other what you think just happened. Do it without yelling. Brian, you go first."

b. First Child's Point of View

Brian then looked at you and said, "I'm mad because…"

You interrupt him, and tell him to talk directly to Emma.

"OK, OK. Emma, you took my trucks away inside the tent, and wouldn't let me play with them."

"How did you feel when that happened, Brian?"

"I felt bad."

Now, Emma, what did Brian say?

"It wasn't that..." Emma replied defensively.

You interrupt Emma, and ask her to say what Brian was saying, in her own words.

"But I needed more..."

You interrupt Emma yet again. "Emma, please tell Brian what *he* just said. Maybe it's what happened, or maybe not. Just tell him in your own words what he said."

Emma sighed, and said, "Brian, you said that I took your trucks and you couldn't play with them."

"And what did he say after that?"

"He said he felt bad."

"Very good, Emma," said Mom. It is very useful and loving to praise a child for understanding clearly what happened, and what feeling was aroused in the other.

c. Second Child's Point of View

"Emma, now it's your turn to tell Brian what happened and how you feel about it," you instructed.

"OK. Brian, I wanted more room to play with my dolls, but then you took them away."

"And how did that make you feel, Emma?"

"I got mad."

"Brian, what did Emma say?"

"But she…" blurted out Brian, looking at you.

Then you interrupt Brian, and instruct him to repeat what Emma said.

"Emma said she needed more room for her dolls, and…uhm…"

Then you coach him. "What did she say she was feeling?"

"She said…"

You interrupt him. "Tell Emma what *she* said she was feeling."

"She said she felt mad."

"Good, Brian. It sounds like you remember what she said and how she felt," Mom remarked. Now the two of you have given the children some positive reinforcement for their listening skills. Those are vital in resolving any conflict.

At that point in the incident there is a "Lose–Lose" dilemma. You want them to come to an understanding about what will work for both of them. The solution lies in one of two options:

- A Compromise, or
- A Win–Win Situation

A Win–Win solution is the ideal one, but a compromise can work too.

Emma and Brian walked into the yard to discuss the issue.

"You could play with your trucks outside of the tent, Brian," she suggested.

"They're small trucks; they won't stand up on the crooked grass."

"WELL, I CAN'T PLAY WITH MY DOLLS ON THE GRASS! THEY'LL FALL DOWN!"

You interceded at that point. "Emma…Brian, now you're both back where you started. This is a situation that has more than one solution."

"Well, I need a flat surface to run my trucks," explained Brian.

"Aren't there any flat surfaces around the yard?" you asked.

"I could play them on the patio by the window."

Then Brian retrieved his trucks from the tent, and set up his motorway on the patio. Emma returned to the tent. "Very good, children," you said. It is important to give positive reinforcement when children deal with conflict, and come up with their own solutions.

Five minutes later, Emma emerged from the tent, and came over to our table for some lemonade. As she sipped on it, she watched Brian play. Shortly thereafter, she came over and played with her dolls on another section of the patio.

You glanced at your wife. She had a small grin on her face. Then she whispered to you, "Now *no one* is playing in the tent!" Then both of you laughed heartedly.

Raising children can be very amusing, even in the worst of times.

5. Peer Pressure

The pressure to conform exerted by society can be overwhelming. You are bombarded with ads, and inundated with knowledge about the latest trends. Long lines at the store queue up waiting for the latest update on a product you already have. Why? Because they said it's great and everybody wants to have one.

a. Who is "THEY?"

As you look at the folks standing in those long lines, what do you see? A line of people wearing jeans and tops…jeans and tops…jeans and tops…and a skirt now and again. You look at them more closely for any individual differences. There are none. It is just a line of people shifting their weight from one leg to the next, or rocking sideways in anticipation. Those people are just nameless faces in a string of faces.

When you go to the first football game at Junior High, you pull out your camera, put on the zoom function, and take a snapshot of your son. Later, you send the picture to your relatives and friends on Facebook. No, not a picture of the whole team; you send the picture of your child. He has something the other team members don't have. He has your love. That is what makes all the difference.

You don't want him to be victimized by all the hollow principles of conformity that are just a set of rules and regulations set forth by an invisible tyrant.

b. The Myth of Conformity

If you and your children conform to certain norms and customs, *then* certain rewards are expected to follow. That is what "They" teach your child. "They" teach him that everybody will admire them if they look and act like everyone else. In reality, children who are obsessed with this adherence to conformity without your guidance, may be sentenced to become just a member of the masses. They are all the same.

Yet, when you reflect upon those who have achieved fame and fortune, it is always because they did something *different.*

Children believe in different, too, but it doesn't mean asserting their individuality. It means "different from you!" This is only the beginning, and you are apprehensive. What will he be like after the storms are past? You don't know, but aren't you curious?

The father of our story remembered some of his experiences well. Brian aspired to be a member of the football team. "All the cool kids play football."

"How do you know that?"

"Because *they* said so." Here, we see the tyrant rising. That's the invisible tyrant known by the name of "They."

After Brian was put on the team, he was very proud. You and he went to the sports equipment store and you spent a small fortune on the protective gear. Once he was totally outfitted in the uniform, he showed you his uniform, and admired himself in the mirror.

Brian was a small boy, but you noted that he ran quite well at the games. Sometimes another team member would pass him the ball, and he dodged and weaved among the larger boys deftly. He also scored a couple of touchdowns, and you cheered with him in victory.

Several months later, Brian came home, dragging his feet. As he sat down for supper, he clenched his chest. "What's wrong, Brian?" you asked.

"Nothing."

"Then why are you holding your chest?"

"I tripped and fell down. That's all." You let that go, until you heard him moaning in pain that night. A trip to the urgent care facility followed that. Brian had a broken rib. Although it took a while and a lot of prodding, he finally complained that he was tackled from behind and all the boys piled on top of him. Prodding may not be your favorite approach, but is sometimes necessary. As a parent, you know that you need to hear "the rest of the story."

Brian was so desperate to become one of the "cool" kids that he was willing to endure pain. Sometimes it is important to let children continue with experimenting, as long as it isn't life threatening.

After a broken ankle, a sprained wrist, and a torn hamstring, you and your wife confronted him. "Is it 'cool' not to be able to play football because you have a cast on?" you asked rhetorically. Pointing out some of his abilities, such as running, you persuaded him to quit football and join track. For a while, you were "Enemy Number One," but that faded in time. Brian often came home raving about Shakir, the boy on his team who excelled.

Memory is useful to employ now. You can remind your child how he thought "cool" kids were admired, but there are other ways of being admired, like Shakir was.

The esteem of others looms large in children's minds. Sports has somehow become the ultimate achievement for boys, in particular. That is also a widely held myth among parents of boys. Consider this story (which is one you might tell your child – regardless of their gender.)

c. Peer Pressure on Parents

Peer pressure isn't merely the ogre that affects pre-teens and teenagers. Peer pressure exists for parents. If you listen to your own adult friends, there are many who spend much time bragging about their children. Then you just sit there, and wonder if you can compete with them. The game of "one up man ship" is one that parents play with each other. If you had a special skill as a child, you might look upon your child and expect something similar to you. Some parents are especially active in conducting defensive maneuvers in order to move their children ahead – as they see it. Some women push their girls to attend beauty contests, or spend a lot of money trying to get them into modeling. Examples of such goals are myriad.

At school, fathers may be forceful in order to push their sons ahead. Reflect on those times when you saw some child's father on the field enmeshed in a loud argument with the coach. For boys, excellence in sports is often considered the ultimate achievement. As parents, you, too, are vulnerable to peer influence. Here is an example of a child who didn't even play sports, and didn't even seem to have a superior skill at all. This is a true story you might share with your children.

Fernando and the Fire

Fernando was thirteen and his parents often asked him to babysit his two little sisters. He was quite good at it, and always contacted you if there was an issue.

However, Fernando only achieved average grades, and sometimes even failed his subjects. He also wasn't good at sports. His parents searched for a special talent or

---

ability, but never found one he excelled at. He was a responsible child, though. So his parents were happy with that and praised him for it.

One day, a fire broke out in your home while Fernando was babysitting. No one knew quite how it started. Fernando was downstairs playing a video game when he first smelled smoke and spotted flames licking from underneath the doorway to the guest bedroom. Instead of yielding to his instincts to run out the front door, he threw an afghan over his head and ran upstairs. Already, the fire had spread to the top of the stairs and bannister. One by one, he struggled to take his sisters downstairs and outside.

After the incident, he had third degree burns on his face and legs, but his sisters were only affected by smoke inhalation.

There are no stars, no certificates, no diplomas, and no trophies for such acts of pure heroism. According to the immortal words of Antoine De Saint-Exupery,

"It is only with the heart that one can see rightly. What is essential is invisible to the eye."

Courage will be demanded of you as your child steps into the initial stages of self-discovery. There are many skirmishes yet to freckle your future. Do pick your battles, as you will wear yourself out if you don't. Unfortunately, peer pressure can tempt your child to smoke, drink, and experiment with drugs. Although your child may roll his eyes when you remind him reassure him that you love him, he will take you up on that when a crisis strikes.

d. Signs and Symptoms

Peer pressure exists. However, obsession with conformity to the "cool" kids will loom large and swallow up your children's time unexpectedly. Some of the symptoms:

- A drop in grades
- Consistently arriving home at late hours
- Mood swings
- Fatigue

- Refusal to tell parents where they are going
- Skipping school
- Anxiety
- Stealing money from home
- Persistent withdrawal from all family activities
- Changes in appetite
- A sudden change in his style of dress or his hairstyle
-

As with your approach for your children when they are young, encourage dialogue and communication. It takes a lot of control on your part to refrain from judgment or criticism, but try.

Make your home a place that welcomes your child's friends. Eavesdrop if possible or make excuses to go into his room. Manifest honest curiosity about the activities he is doing with his friends. Then leave. Above all, avoid being what is called a "helicopter parent." That is one who constantly patrols their children and makes decisions for them.

6. Bullying

Oddly enough, bullies are often children who lack self-esteem. Their bullying behavior represents an attempt to overcompensate by substituting power for esteem. Society in the 21st century promotes competition as a road to success. There are some, though, who shy away from competition toward a laudable goal and develop maladjusted ways of feeling successful. Instead of taking up the gauntlet and competing with others, they deviously try to use intimidation – rather than competition – as a means of "feeling good." Have you ever noticed how a bully singles out one or two other children? Bullies find it an exhausting self-imposed challenge to take on a crowd. While they may relish a group of onlookers, they will never confront all of them. After all, why turn off one's misguided "fans?" What's more, have you ever noticed that a bully's victims are usually smaller than he is?

a. Early Parental Guidance and Modeling

You have encouraged your child to share his experiences with you. In addition, you have taught him to be aware and empathic. He is sensitive to the feelings of another. It's essential that you, as a parent, inform your children of these bullying possibilities. Tell them to inform you of any such behaviors, reminding him that this is not "tattle-telling," or a sign of weakness.

Parental behavior serves as a model for children, although the preteen or teenager would never admit that. It is poor practice to use swear words in front of children, even if you tell them not to use them. A sure-fire way of doing that is to eliminate it from your own conversations with other adults.

b. Appeal to Authority

Teachers and principals of schools are very protective of the children. It is a natural parental instinct present not only in human beings, but in all mammals. In fact, it is so strong that an authority figure may even bend or break their own rules to protect the children. They will even scapegoat themselves based on the higher good. Consider this true-life example:

Mrs. Ramen's Raid

In a middle class school, the children always had regularly scheduled lavatory breaks. One day in the Fall of the year, Mrs. Ramen, a teacher, announced lavatory period. Most of the boys stayed seated. "Don't you need to visit the bathroom like you usually do?" They said they didn't need to go. She shrugged her shoulders and continued the lesson after the girls and a few boys returned.

For the next couple of days, the same phenomenon happened. As she was walking down the aisle explaining the lesson one day, she noticed that Emil had a cut on his forehead. He explained that it didn't hurt, he didn't want to see the nurse, and it just happened when he fell in the bathroom. "To the nurse, Emil," she said forcefully.

Now, Mrs. Ramen was a gentle woman and abided by all the standards and practices laid down by the school for teacher conduct. However, this time was different.

Suddenly, she flew down the hall and kicked open the swinging door to the boys' room — a big no-no in terms *of appropriate conduct.*

Two boys were standing in the center of the room and were shocked by her entry. She stood with her arms folded blocking the doorway. Trapped in there, they looked at her in shock and horror.

"Hey! You don't belong here," said the larger boy defiantly.

With equal defiance, she replied, "So?"

"This is the boys room," he said.

"I noticed," she responded.

"...But you're a woman!"

"I've noticed that too."

"You guys belong at the urinals, in the stalls, at the sink, or back in your classrooms," she continued, as she stepped aside from the door. The two boys then slinked out. Already there were several boys peeking into the doorway watching. She didn't know if she had interrupted a bullying episode or not, but she knew the

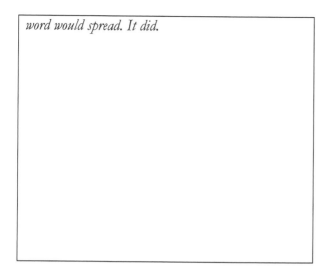

word would spread. It did.

Violent rites of passage belong to the primitive people many eons ago. They should not be tolerated in civilized cultures.

Society has a curious way of centering their cultures around a central point of activity. In the early days, it was the marketplace, where children participated along with their parents. Later on, the heart of society was found in the activities of the craft guilds, where youngsters worked as junior apprentices. The factories and industrial centers later replaced those, but – alas – children were forced to work at a very young age. Today, the center of activity for children is the school.

121

The son featured in this book was victimized by a bully, and Dad taught him how to deal with it. Of course, Dad could have intervened, but he preferred that his son, Brian, learn to deal with himself, if possible. That is usually the most ideal solution.

One day, Dad came home and noticed that Brian looked disheveled and was wearing a dirty and flimsy windbreaker rather than his nice new warm jacket with the logo of his football team on it. Although it took while and a bit of prodding for you to ferret the full story out of him:

"Brian, where's your football jacket?"

"Uhm...I left it in my locker."

"Your clothes are all messed up, too," you remarked, suspecting that he may have been bullied, but reluctant to share that with you.

"I was just playing."

"Where's that laptop I gave you for your work?"

"Uhm...I left it at school."

"In your locker?" you asked. "Let's drive back there and get it. You need it for your homework."

"I don't have any homework today."

You were silent, knowing that Brian had homework every night except weekends. This was just Wednesday.

"I'm going to drive you back to the school, and we'll get your jacket and laptop anyhow."

"*NO!* Don't do that!" Brian begged.

"Grab a warm jacket, Brian, and get in the car. The janitor will let you go to your locker and get them." you added.

"They're not in my locker!" Brian admitted. Then he started crying.

After holding him and hugging him, you softened your voice and asked, "Brian what *really* happened?"

"Uhm...this kid, Harley, took them."

"And you let him?" you asked.

"No. But that's how my clothes got messed up. He was pushing and hollering, but took them anyway. I couldn't stop him; he's too strong."

"Did you tell one of the teachers?" you inquired.

"*NO! NO!* You can't do that. After the fuss blows over, Harley will come back again – madder than ever!"

"Does he look at you and holler threats?" you asked.

"Yup. He stands there face-to-face and yells till I do what he wants. He says he's going be beat me up if I don't."

"Here's what you can try, Brian, if you're brave enough. I know you can be brave when you make up your mind."

Brian looked up at you, but was till racked with worry. So, you continued:

"Brian, the next time he faces you and starts his yelling routine, just stand there and listen. Focus intently upon the bridge of his eyes. When you do that, it appears to the other person that you're looking at both of their eyes. Then slowly glide your glance all over the skin on his face. Look for a bump or a freckle on it, or any kind of flaw. Everybody has them."

"Why should I do that?" Brian asked, but you continued without explanation.

"After you spot a bump or mark on his face, point to it. You can say something like, 'What's that bump?' or 'What's that mark?' or describe whatever it is, and ask him about it."

"Next, mention that your Dad had a mark like that once and still has the stuff he used to get rid of it. Assure him, it works great! More than likely, he'll go along with that."

"What's the stuff, Dad?"

"It won't hurt him. I'll get it for you later."

After supper, you went to your wife and explained the situation, along with the possible solution. Then you asked her to check out her cosmetics. She then located some foundation cream, mixed it with a dollop of lotion, and placed the mixture in a very small unmarked container. Afterwards, you presented it to Brian. "Don't tell anyone else about it. It's a secret."

"What's that stuff?"

"Never mind, Brian. It won't hurt him. Tell him he needs to apply just a tiny bit if it on daily, but it may take a little while to work."

Brian did that and reported back the next day.

"Dad, I saw him in the boy's room. He was looking at his chin in the mirror. That's where the tiny little bump is. Then I gave him the stuff. He seemed happy about it."

"If he approaches you again, ask him if the stuff is working. Mention that it may take some time. That will distract him from the harassment. If he returns again, find some weakness or slight flaw. If for instance, he doesn't run that fast, you can suggest running a few yards with him on the school track. Do that when there are other people around. Keep it up, until he leaves you alone. Never volunteer to do his homework for him or help him cheat. Just say you're not good on that subject."

Because bullies psychologically have very low self-esteem, they are likewise very conscious of their appearance. That is why Harley of the story bought into the ruse. Harley also had poor motor coordination, even though he was large. That may have been why the football jacket was of great interest to him. Theft of the laptop was caused by a need to feel he had manipulated you. That gave him a sense of perverted pleasure.

c. The Myth of Permanence

Because children spend so much time at school, that environment and those fellow classmates become take on an aura of permanence. In their minds, they subtly believe that all those other children will always be there forevermore. Even if you happen to take them to a college with your older child, your son or daughter will picture themselves there along with all the same classmates they have today, or at least, copies of them. Children live in a narrow environment – home – school – home –school and so on *ad nauseam.* Yet there is a myriad of opportunities for them to participate in activities totally removed from the school environment. Although it may cost more in terms of parents' time and money, membership in civic or private groups or organizations can provide multivariate options. Activities that are disciplined, have smaller groups, and build a child's confidence can offer a respite from the constant pressures of interactions with the same children. For boys, martial arts programs such as karate or a lesser known one called Bushido, the various styles of Tai Chi, 4-H Clubs, Scouts, Junior Explorer Clubs, horseback riding schools, bands sponsored by the town or region, choral groups, and the Police Athletic League in America can help your son build confidence. Such groups are closely supervised, and proper etiquette and behavior are demanded. Individual attention is present, as the leaders have the opportunity to help each child personally to be successful and achieve the task at hand. Bullies would never survive in such an atmosphere.

The myth of permanence is broken by the fact that there is something more in their young lives beside the school and home. There's a whole new world full of new ambitious and adventuresome children just a few miles from home.

CHAPTER 6: DISCIPLINE

Every parent knows that the home would become a battle zone without discipline. Instilling discipline in your child will make your life easier and you would be able to enjoy your children. In addition, your child benefits. He learns that there are rewards and gratifications he can receive if he is able to function well at home, in school, and in his environment. As an adult, a person who isn't self-controlled – at least to some extent – is left without a job or money.

Human survival depends upon it. Indeed, all sentient species learn some degree of discipline. In the animal kingdom, it may come in the form of the development of a learned skill, like hunting. For some animals, discipline is necessary to interact with others of the same species. That way, they will enlist the support of the group in order to hunt, eat, have shelter, and even secure the love of their mates. Rules of conduct are essential.

Even the Groundhogs Have Ground Rules

One evening in late spring a couple was in their living room enjoying a TV show. It was early evening. Suddenly, an odd animal sound came from the garden outside their front door. They knew there was a groundhog hole just behind their majestic Rhododendron, and that seemed to be the source of the noise. Groundhog families of the creatures grew up there every season. The couple maintained a state of peaceful co-existence with the animals.

After hearing the yelping sound yet again, the wife rushed out to investigate. Everything was quiet when she first arrived, so she stood at the garden's edge and waited. Then little barks, rustling noises, and sounds of movement emitted from the hole. At once, Great Mother Groundhog climbed out of the hole, turned around and stared at it. The little barks continued. Her baby groundhogs were restless and battled with each other for a preferred position. Mother Groundhog then mustered her own commanding voice and barked loudly into the hole. The restlessness then ceased.

Even the lowly rodents correct their children, knowing that their survival in the future depends upon cooperation with others. It also provided her and her

1. The "Rule of Big"

When your children are infants, they instinctively know that you provide them with their basic needs. They will happily accept what you can do for them. Love and affection are also one of those needs, as the father of our book realized when his boy's physical needs had been met, but he kept crying. He needed to be held, rocked, and caressed.

When his child reached about 1 ½, he developed the muscular ability to manipulate objects. Naturally, he exercised it. One afternoon, Mom had him play on the floor of the kitchen with his little plush animals and plastic toys. These he moved around and developed little "pathways" on his blankets like roads for his toys and moved them about. Mom then stepped into the pantry closet to gather some food for supper. Upon her return, her son had migrated to a lower kitchen cabinet and had pots and pans spread all over the floor. She then had to perform an act of discipline, but gently to allow for his level of immaturity. Moms, of course, are much larger than their children. Use the advantage of size to control your child, but do so gently.

So, patiently, Mom stood way above her little boy. He looked up and saw her figure looming over him. Very importantly, she accompanied this action with voice, but it was not a shout. It was firm. "No, Brian. Those are Moms. Yours are over there," she said, pointing to his toys.

Then she carefully picked him up and moved him back to his designated play area. Naturally, he cried but got over it quickly.

Brian was merely learning to control and manipulate his environment but needed to learn there were boundaries. What the mother was addressing was his behavior, but was also invoking his higher brain centers.

This is the process to which the psychologists, Seigel and Payne call "Integration the Left and Right Brain." That is, integrating the experimental, free-wheeling self (the right brain) with a primary level of cognition (the left brain).

Actually, the terms "Right-Brained" and "Left-Brained" are not physical locations within the brain. However, some use these concepts to distinguish between the creative aspects of a person and the logical aspects of that person. In order to be well-adjusted, everyone needs to integrate and use both aspects of their brains. Some will tend to favor the more logical aspects of their minds; others will tend to favor the more creative aspects. Our mathematicians and scientists will tend to favor logic, while our innovators and artists prefer to use new techniques or create beauty and entertainment.

2. The Role of the Emotions

In the story above when little Brian decided to play with the pots and pans rather than his own toys, his Mother corrected him gently. He cried at first. Because he was being directed to do something he did not want to do, he became upset and angry. Brian was now learning that he was not always in control of his self-proclaimed "universe."

We are now in an area neither governed by the "right brain," *nor* by the "left brain." Siegel and Payne call the emotional center of the brain the "downstairs" brain. In Chapter 3, this book discusses this with reference to the physiological area, the amygdala, which actually is in the lower brain. Thought and logic emanate from the higher frontal lobe of the brain, the neo cortex. This area directs thought. Siegel et. al. call that area the "upstairs brain."

Having been discouraged from playing with the pots and pans, Brian had now moved into the pantry closet. Mom was busy browning some beef and didn't notice right away. In his typically organized fashion, Brian had some boxes lined up together, with some cans lined up neatly next to them. Then he picked up a can of soup and thrust it down on top of a box of noodles. *Smash!* She ran over to the pantry. "No, Brian," she said. "No!" Children hate "No's." So instead of stopping, Brian rammed the can into more boxes. Just then Dad came home.

Instead of his usual loving greeting, Dad was met by a raucous *Smash! Smash! Smash!* followed by his own hollering at the arrival of Mom. She was anxious to return to her frying, as the meat was beginning to burn. Emma had come upon the scene and stood there laughing, and Brian hollered even louder. Now the whole family was in their tiny kitchen.

Brian was in the throes of intense emotion, and appeal to his "upstairs brain," or his logic centers at that time would be ineffective. The "downstairs brain" drowned out engagement into thought and logic.

"Brian," said Dad. "Would you like to go outside and smash things out there?" Brian liked that idea. Of course, Dad was wondering what item would be suitable, as he didn't want his garden to be destroyed. He then arranged piles of the little stones below some of the plants. Handing his son a small rock, he had Brian smash down the piles. Emma came out to help. It helped her feel good to be of help in the exercise, so she formed tempting piles of white stones. It worked. Brian giggled and laughed. His anger was diverted into a harmless activity.

Two things happened during this exercise:

Sublimation

Energy Release

Sublimation is a redirection of one's impulses into less destructive and more productive channels. It is a defense mechanism used throughout maturity as well. Very subtly, the father wanted his child to find more socially acceptable ways to express his desires. This is far, far better than repressing one's feelings. When one represses a feeling, it has physical and emotional ramifications. If a person gets tense and has no appropriate outlet for the emotion of anger, he may endure gastric ailments as result. Psychologically, he may become bitter, resentful, and frustrated with life in general.

Energy Release is also essential to expel the effects of the hormone adrenaline that is released during anger episodes. When a person is angry, muscles tighten and the body is ready for action. Adrenaline builds up in one's system until it is used up through physical release. When anger is repressed and not redirected to some acceptable form of action, it produces glucose

137

in the system. Too much glucose converts into glycogen which is eventually stored as body fat.

3. Structure and Schedule

While you want your children to be well-behaved, you do not want to rule them with an iron fist. That only serves to produce fear and lack of trust on the part of your child. You want your child to share with you stories about what causes them stress and what arouses their negative emotions. You want to accept the fact that they have feelings, and that is OK. However, it is what they do about those feelings that makes the difference. Therefore, open communication is necessary in order to help your child interpret and integrate those feelings with their logic and higher brain functions. That will not happen in a chaotic environment at home, in school, or when interacting with others. This is not an uncommon experience with some parents who were unprepared for the obligations of parenting. Here is an example:

Freda, the Frazzled Parent

Freda as at the stove furiously cooking up a meat sauce for her lasagna. Her husband and his brother were stopping by for supper with her and her children. Eric came into the kitchen and grabbed some cookies. "Eric," said his mother, "Go out and play with your friends until I call you for supper. He ran out the door at top speed. Shortly afterward, Eric came rushing back with a few friends to get his soccer ball. They laughed and talked at a holler as they rifled through his room searching for the ball. Freda was already feeling agitated as the sauce was slow to heat up. "STOP YELLING!" she shouted. "ERIC, GO STUDY IN YOUR ROOM!" That made no sense to Eric because she had just told him to go outside to play. He and his friends exchanged puzzled glances. Then Eric leaped up with the soccer ball he dug out of his closet and ran back outside. "BE BACK IN TIME FOR SUPPER!" bellowed Freda. Eric had no idea when that would happen and was confused because she said she'd call for him. So, he and the boys ran back outside. Soccer, of course, was preferred over studying. After her husband and his brother arrived along with her teenage son, Eric wasn't there. Freda asked, "Now, where is that boy of mine?" Freda asked. She then went over to the window, opening it wide and shouted, "ERIC! IT'S TIME FOR SUPPER! COME HOME!" The neighbor was walking his new dog and the poor animal strained at his leash trying to scamper into the street in fright. Freda served her husband, his brother, her other son and everyone engaged in lively conversation. Fifteen minutes later, Eric and two of his friends came in. "This is Darryl and Tom. Can they have supper too?" Freda just nodded. Then she set up for them, and they joined the table. Now, instead of five people for supper, there were seven.

Eric never got his homework done that day, nor did he on many other days. Consequently, he didn't get good grades in school. When his mother and father spoke to him regarding the issue, he agreed to study more but had no reliable structure upon which to rely for accomplishing the task. Furthermore, he didn't understand how nor why it happened. It was one of many times he didn't understand the connection between his lack of effort and the results. His parents had never given him the lesson of consequences. Yet the

A child, and even an adult needs a structure and a secure place in which he can express himself and accomplish his tasks. Furthermore, he desperately needs to be able to predict results if he demonstrates various kinds of behaviors. Regardless of whether or not those results are positive or negative, there is security in having some notion as to what those results might be.

If he does something praiseworthy, a child should be praised and lauded for doing so. Likewise, if he does something that is clearly wrong, at least he feels secure in knowing the most likely consequences. You will not disown him if he breaks something of yours in anger.

On the other hand, if you simply let them express those feelings and hope that they learn the "hard way," you might be opening them out to be hurt by those who resist, or lead them to compensate by being even more aggressive.

141

Although it took several minor skirmishes, the father of this book was able to institute a schedule. Brian's first duty upon his arrival home from school was to get a snack and then retire to his room to do his homework. When there was football practice or other related activities the times were shifted around. His mom assiduously kept a large calendar full of boxes for each day of the month. On it, the times for his practice were delineated.

After a short time, Brian adhered to the schedule on a regular basis without question. He learned how to check the schedule as often as Mom. If he needed help with homework, Mom or Dad obliged. This regimen gave him a sense of security because he recognized that it would lead to success. His grades were fairly good as result. Therefore, he felt secure in his home environment and felt the rewards of his efforts. This was a win-win situation.

It sounds simple, doesn't it? Not so fast. Nothing in life is entirely predictable. Otherwise, life would be rather boring and lack challenge. Stuff happens.

One day, Brian came slinking into the house. He didn't even want his snack and went up to his room in total silence. By the time Dad got home, Brian was on his cell phone complaining loudly to a classmate.

"She's got some nerve!" he shouted to his friend over the phone. "It's just not fair! Why is she always picking on me?" Dad then entered his room. It was obvious Brian wasn't doing his homework as usual because his unopened backpack had been flung on his bed.

"I gotta' go, Larry," said Brian and abruptly shut off the phone. Then he leaned on his desk with his back turned.

"What's wrong, Brian?" asked Dad.

"Nothin'," he replied. Dad then moved in closer and stood alongside him silently waiting. "Aw' right…Aw' right. I'll tell you."

Dad could see that Brian was upset and angry. The first objective of creating an open relationship with your child is to solicit his feelings, label them, and understand the reasons behind them.

"Dad, that new English teacher is always bugging me! Then she tells me to stop, and go up to the page in the book we're talking about. Right in front of the class, she corrects me! She does that to me, never to the other kids." *Never?* You asked yourself silently.

Now you want to help him label his feeling. "How does that make you feel, Brian?"

"I get mad. She doesn't like me. She's just plain *mean!*"

"I can understand you might be embarrassed that you feel like you're being singled out." Now, however, you want him to engage his higher brain functions in order to develop a workable solution. In order to do that, you need to find out the rest of the story. "How come your teacher asked you to 'go up' to the page the class was looking at?"

"Well, I was on the wrong page by then."

"How come?"

Silence.

"Brian, how come you weren't following along with the lesson?"

"Uhm...I was poking Andrew. You should see how he reacts when you poke him! His shoulders shoot up and he jerks. I catch him by surprise. Then all the kids laugh."

"How do you think the teacher feels when that happens?"

"She's annoyed, I guess."

"Do you think maybe you disrupted the class?"

"Yeah...but it's funny, Dad."

"It sounds like it might be, Brian. But what is the purpose of being in the class?"

"Yeah...I know...I know. It's to learn."

It helps to weave an imaginary scenario for your son or play a game which would help him see and appreciate another's feelings and be successful in the long haul.

Brian, suppose you were a cave explorer and you were showing twenty people a cave that you knew very well. It was your job to lead them through all the many, many passageways in the cave without getting lost. How would you go about it?"

"I'd lead them."

"If they didn't all follow you, what would happen?"

"Some would get lost."

"Now you have a problem, don't you?"

"Uh, huh."

After this, you decided to discuss various solutions for the problem. After that, you complicated the dilemma by remarking to Brian, "What if you were able to find most of the people but not all of them?"

"Uh, oh," replied Brian.

"Every puzzle does not have a perfect solution."

Once you concluded the game with its unsettling result, Brian's father drew in the analogy he created.

146

"So, if your teacher is trying to teach a lesson to her students, and your sideline activities interrupted her, perhaps some of the children wouldn't learn the lesson – maybe including you."

Parents and children become closer when the child is given an interesting dilemma to solve. It is a more appropriate way to handle not only your own reaction to your child's misbehavior but also teach your child to utilize his higher brain to understand his teacher's reaction and to overcome his own anger.

Without the necessity of imposing of penalty, your child has learned more about his behavior and that of his teacher. Hence, there is an integration of his higher brain over his emotional array.

Even so, children will deviate from your guidelines, especially preteens and teens. Encourage them to dialogue with you, if they become nervous or afraid. Children have difficulty discriminating between what is true or untrue, safe or dangerous. That only comes with maturity and emotional intelligence.

4. Social Networking Sites (SNS)

For preteens and teens, these are the favorite social sites in their order of usage:

1. Instagram

2. Twitter

3. Facebook

4. Pinterest

5. Tumblr

6. Google+

7. Reddit

8. Snapchat

Similarly, there are real-time apps, chat programs and online sites popular among that age group. Most require a minimum age of 13 or 18 in some cases, but underage children find easy ways to by bypass that:

1. Ask.fm

2. Down

3. Fess

4. Kik Messenger

5. MeetMe

6. Oovoo

7. Periscope

8. Tango

9. uMentioned

10. Undernet

11. Vine

12. WhatsApp

13. Whisper.sh

14. Yik Yak

The older programs originated in the business world and colleges in the 1990's. They were located on Gopher servers that restricted entry. Nevertheless, it was relatively simple for others to enter them and benefit. One could use them for file storage, to play games, engage in real-time chat, or download applications from them for free.

The intent of the software developers today is to gain popularity, and eventually make money. Hence there are functions that easily allow abuse, because that attracts even more followers. Children are free to tell secrets, engage in cyber bullying, and be victimized by trolls and even sexual predators. Anarchy rages in these places.

However, productive and informational items are also posted. Games and quiz-styled interactions run by a "bot" (robot server) also are present.

Children can create monikers or avatars that they feel typifies their personality. OR they can create a user name that represents exactly who they are *not*." Skeletor" can really be a fat kid creating an illusion of strength and power, or it could be a sexually deviant 44-year old.

Regardless of whether your child is honest and forthright or not, the digital screen provides a mask. Your child will feel a false sense of safety because he's virtually anonymous. That is its greatest lure. Others can say anything they want, without the fear that their listeners will come to the door of their homes and repeat it person-to-person to the listener.

On the Internet, everyone can hide behind a screen. While you spent so much time and effort to teach your child courtesy, and a sense of awareness of the feelings of others, even the most respectful child may flush that fact down the drain. Your children can and will separate their praiseworthy conduct from that of the Internet.

a. **The Dark Web**

Yes, you've heard of that. It exists. However, there is a "darker" web surreptitiously present. It leaps up through a link mentioned in a chat program or discussion group. Usually it disappears within a week, so the people responsible can avoid detection. A new site will crop up to replace it and likewise vanish quickly. Be aware that your kids may explore those darker places.

Internet safety is a buzz phrase used these days. It is an attempt to institute protocols to guard young people and the vulnerable. However, it won't really work on many occasions. Parenting is a risky affair, but you can only do the best you can. Trust your children, but give them warnings. They may choose to disregard those warnings, especially during the teenage years, but will revert to your standards later on.

b. Real People behind the Pixels

The father of our story here had several enlightening experiences when he first watched his son, Brian, converse with a girl. The conversation was innocent and light. They talked about what schools each attended and their interests. You, as the father, watched with interest. Just then, Mom called upstairs to announce supper. Suddenly, Brian clicked on the "X," and left the chat program.

"Hey! What happened to that girl?" you asked.

"She saw me leave."

"Brian, she didn't *see* you leave. All of sudden, you were gone."

"Yeah, that's how it works."

"Yes, but that's not how a human being 'works'. People just don't beam out, like on a sci-fi show."

Brian laughed.

"Just like you, that girl is a real person with real feelings. How do you think she felt when you abruptly left? Did she feel like laughing like you just did?"

"Dunno'."

"Of course you don't know, but I certainly don't think she laughed. Maybe she felt bad. Maybe others have done the same thing to her, and she felt really depressed. When I leave someone's house, I say 'Good-bye" at least. It would sure look silly if I just leaped up and ran out of their house. They would feel slighted, or figure that I'm just plain rude or stupid."

c. Unreal People behind the Pixels

On one occasion, the father of our story was approached by his son announcing he wanted lessons in Taebo Kickboxing. Well, he was small but wiry so that sounded interesting.

"How did you find out about that, Brian?" you asked.

"This army kid on the Internet. He said he saw my picture and thought I could develop some muscles, after I learned a little kickboxing. Look..."

You looked at the profile picture of the young man who contacted him. He was in military fatigues. The face looked familiar but you couldn't quite place it. Then you read the conversation on your son's cell phone. It raved on about the wonders of kickboxing, and the young man added that he lived nearby, and that Brian and he could meet someday. This you found unsettling. After you did some research, you came across a photo in a newspaper, and spoke to your son again.

"Brian, I know who that guy is," you said. "He's not who he says he is."

"He isn't? Who is he then?" Brian asked.

"His profile picture is that of a soldier who died ten months ago."

"Why is he doing this?"

"I don't know, Brian, but it's nothing good."

Children unfortunately are gullible, and may believe things are true only because they're on the Internet. Warn your children, and suggest that no one can be entirely trustworthy, even friends or an apparently reliable source.

d. The Longevity of Words and Photos on Social Media and other Internet Sites

All of you know that you can go back to remarks you've made several years ago still lingering there in Cyberspace. Many have failed to get jobs because a potential employer visited their Facebook page, only to find a picture of them at a drinking orgy…or worse. Even material that is "deleted" might be retrieved.

5 Research and Learning Tools

The Internet can be informational and educational as well as entertaining. You can instruct your children as to how to use Wikipedia, Internet dictionaries, online libraries, discussion groups, forums, and teachers' web sites. Stick with the moderated groups for the most part. You child could benefit greatly and obtain information for essays, term papers, and the pursuit of intellectual interests. Plagiarism and cheating can be easily detected, though. Many students have been expelled from college for those offenses. Appeal to their higher brains to help your children use their logical abilities.

Glenn's History Award

Glenn was in his freshman year in high school. He was an intelligent boy, and very creative in his approach to his studies. When he was tasked with a long history term paper, he wanted to produce something unique. So, he explored the Internet extensively and came upon the site of a Canadian college professor and author. The professor had a link to his blog posts, but indicated permission was needed to read them and contribute follow-up questions and comments. Glenn composed a carefully worded email letter. This impressed the professor who gave him access.

On the blogs, Glenn found information and material quoted from books that otherwise would have cost him a lot of money. As result of his research, Glenn presented a paper about chivalry in the Middle Ages. His teacher had never read such an extraordinary term paper and Glenn was given an award at the end of the year.

6 Cyberbullying

Many children, and even adults on occasion, are victimized by bullying on the Internet. Bullying requires three kinds of participants: the intimidator, the victim, and the onlookers. The world of cyberspace is inundated with all three. Cyber bullying is often characterized by foul language, insults, teasing, and provocative speech.

One day, Brian, the boy of this book approached his father.

"Dad, check this out." He then showed you a long discussion between himself and another boy in his school —

- "ughh ur so stupid, everybody HATES u wish you would switch schools."
- "I'm not stupid!"
- "just go away, you dirty piece of @#$%!"
- "I thought we were friends …"
- "ur a loser btw how much do u way? 5 pounds?"
- "LOL thaz not so…"

"party at my house guess who isn't invited…you wouldn't be seen any who turn sideways u disappear…"

"Brian," you said, "Just drop him from your list."

"But, Dad, all the kids are laughing at me. I'm not really that skinny. They think he won the argument."

"They think he won because he's nastier; not because he's right."

Unless the problem becomes extreme, parents should not handle the situation for their children. Like boomerangs, bullies always return. It is far better to talk to your kids, ask them how you can help, and teach them that they can control the situation. Depending upon the circumstances, your child might talk to the other student face-to-face, but do so in a public place where there are adults or much older children present.

Encourage your children to participate in off-line confidence-building activities. As indicated in earlier chapters, remind your child about his own "bully brain" that is trying to push him into a hasty reaction.

Suggest that he doesn't try to defend himself. That just baits a bully further. Act like it doesn't bother him, and bring up an unrelated topic. Then leave the conversation, and block his entry if that particular site has techniques for doing so.

Educate your children as to how control their privacy settings on Facebook and other sites. Inform them to change their passwords every couple of months, and never tell anyone – even their closest friends – their passwords.

7   Celebrity Worship

Although the interest in pop music is enhanced by the Internet, it is also a way for celebrities to publicize themselves. That is healthy and normal, unless it becomes an obsession. Lynn McCutcheon first coined the term "celebrity worship" in the early 21st century. In its extreme form, it is and psychological maladjustment. When children, preteens and teenagers become engaged in studying the personal life of a celebrity, they may merely be attracted to sites about that celebrity because of their skills, fame, wealth, and success. When and if it becomes an obsession, they may get sucked into fantasies about that person.

The film director, Martin Scorsese said, "You really get to love them. They don't know you. But you love them. But you love, I think, is what you imagine they are…they represent a dream. You lose yourself in these people."

Advertisers, publicists, and politicians often use celebrities as role models. Preteens and teens are vulnerable to this. The motive is usually money.

Some singers and celebrities speak about drugs and alcohol, accentuating the "fun-filled" effects of usage. They can be deluded into believing that these addictions aren't serious because their favorite idol does it, or did it.

Celebrity worship stems from poor self-esteem. Boosting a child's self-esteem is essential, particularly in their formative years. Although you may feel it's like spying, it is useful to occasionally review the browser histories to determine if your child is becoming obsessed.

One young person said on the Internet, "Celebrities deserve adoration!" Take note of that, consider the healthy upbringing of your children, and do what you can to prevent your children from celebrity worship. Even though celebrities have a bigger platform than yours, your platform is closer.

CHAPTER 7: WHEN THE WARM FRONT MEETS THE COLD FRONT – THE TEMPEST OF THE TEENS

1. Allowing Children to Fail Sometimes

The father in our book was out at a restaurant with his wife, her sister, brother-in-law, and their daughter, Emma. Dad's cell phone rang. It was Brian, now 17. He had his driver's license now and was on a toll highway.

"Dad! I can't pay the toll! I don't have any money on me. Can you some and give me some money or something?"

"I'm forty miles away, Brian."

"Well, can't you just put it into my debit card account? There's nothing in there."

"Brian, the parkway doesn't take debit cards."

"Oh, that's right. But they're gonna' take a picture of my license plate and maybe send me a ticket."

"But, Dad, you gotta' help me!" he whined. "No, Brian. I don't 'gotta' do anything. Your Mom and I are enjoying a pleasant dinner with your aunt and uncle. In fact, you're supposed to be here."

"Uhm…What am I going to do?"

"You're going to go through the toll booth, get a ticket, and pay it."

"But I don't have the money."

"You used to earn it, Brian, but you quit your job at the grocery store."

Brian moaned.

"Our lawn needs mowing, Brian. I'll pay you for that instead of our grass cutter," you said.

Silence.

"Brian?"

"Yeah, OK, I guess."

Here the father is letting his son fail and recognize that there are consequences. However, if you'll notice, he gave his son a way out. It wasn't a dead end street. There are always a number of solutions to a problem, although some are not the most desirable.

2. They Will Rebel – Helping Teens Make Positive Choices

Teens are in that stage of life when they will test the principles you so fervently instilled in them as they were growing up. Because they need to establish their own personhood, they will test those principles to see if they are really valid in their own lives. You are "old-fashioned," in their minds. You don't keep up with the trends that they think will impress others and secure the esteem from others, they think.

You, as the mature adult realize that keeping up with the trends isn't a means of obtaining the esteem of others. The esteem of others is freely *given by the others*. It comes from the perception of who they are as people, not a trend. This is a hard lesson for them to learn and it will take years for them to entirely grasp it.

Jay and the Rap Artist

Jay was very skilled in computer programming and took courses at high school that related to that. He desperately wanted to create applications, and start his own enterprise to promote and sell them. His teachers told him that his work was unique. To further his ambitions, he followed all the recent trends. His parents supported him in this.

During his explorations, Jay got sidetracked and took an interest in rap. He heard about a concert to be presented by a rap artist in the city, and he wanted to go. He asked his girlfriend to accompany him, but she refused to do, so he went there with a friend. He didn't tell his parents either. His parents always instructed him to talk to them first about where he was going, but he knew they would disapprove. 'They didn't understand the trends,' he thought.

However, what his parents really knew was the fact that Jay tended to be easily influenced. He wasn't quite mature enough to distinguish between reality and entertain for entertainment's sake alone.

In his act, this rap artist used a lot of street slang, cast out insults to politicians and celebrities, and words that advocated violence toward women. knew his parents would disapprove of the trip. Jay went anyway. He became enamored of the style, and continued to follow that artist on YouTube videos and purchased many of his albums.

Due to his exposure to this kind of entertainment, Jay adopted the lingo of that rap artist, and peppered his speech liberally with those terms. Once he slung a few shocking insults at his girlfriend, she broke up with him, and threatened a law suit.

What's more, he was expelled from high school for such remarks. His dreams of becoming a software engineer were practically eradicated. He became very

Parents – all too frequently – are left with the chance to help their teens after something very negative happens. If parents have done all they can to keep the channels of communication and dialogue open, their children will seek help from them. It comes in the form of a rescue. When teens are forced to live with a consequence for a negative choice, it is then that their children will realize that the principles they have learned growing up are correct. This is a truly humbling experience for them. Parent will be challenged because of their own anger, which they must sublimate. These experiences often provide the greatest opportunity to show parental love for a child.

The heroes of our story here had a similar experience related to alcohol.

One day, Brian's father got a phone call late at night. It was Brian. Brian again was late for his curfew, but the call had nothing to do with tardiness.

"Dad?"

"Brian, what happened? Where are you?" you asked.

"Uhm…I've been arrested, Dad. Can you post bail for me?"

You gulped, and mustered up the courage to ask, "What were you arrested for?"

"Underage drinking and drunk driving."

You didn't hear any slur in his voice, but sensed that he had been shaken into sobriety by the trauma. Your emotions swelled up and you wanted to holler at him, but kept your cool.

"Which police station?" you asked.

You went over there and bailed him out.

"They impounded my car, too," he said. You just nodded, knowing that Brian would have to earn the money so it could be redeemed. In addition, you and your wife would have to agree to take responsibility for him in order that he could be released in your custody. Also, the two of you would have to bring the car back home. People with DWI charges are not allowed to drive. There was a hearing on the matter. To demonstrate your love and support of your son, you and your wife attended. At result of the hearing, Brian had his license suspended for six months. That upset him greatly, as he would have to arrange for rides from his sister or from friends and neighbors.

a. Why Teens May Make Poor Decisions

Biologically, the brain of an adolescent hasn't completely formed. The center for rational thought is the prefrontal cortex, that is large segment located just behind the forehead. When the prefrontal cortex isn't entirely developed, it affects the areas of the brain that also make rational decisions based upon foresight about the consequences of their behavior. Speaking about the functions of the prefrontal cortex, Dr. Michelle Brennan of Rutgers University has said, "These functions include attention, the ability to regulate emotions, plan/organize, logic, reason, the ability to inhibit impulses (verbal/behavioral), problem-solving, ability to multi-task, and working memory." Because these skills haven't been

170

sufficiently developed, adolescents fail to predict consequences. They may not, for example, foresee that their experiments with drugs may result in the necessity to go into a rehabilitation unit. Somehow, they are given to fantasy and believe that the same cause-effect phenomena don't apply to them. Hence, they break a lot of rules.

3. Peer Pressure, Alcohol, and Drugs

Because of the information explosion, there is no fail-safe method of getting your teen to avoid the toxic relationships that reinforce his negative choices. In order for him to select positive friends, he himself needs to be gently led to select those who have similar goals for themselves in life. Some of those goals may have to do with:

- Career
- Mastery of skill
- Interests
- Monetary success
- Emotional Intelligence

- Social skills
- Love relationships

Teens have an oversensitive fear of rejection, of being ridicules, of hurting someone's feelings, of being disliked. Many simply don't know how to extract themselves from situations that can lead them into negative behaviors. It is extremely difficult for them to develop what is called "Refusal Skills." As parents you can't do that for them. Encourage them to develop them for themselves according to their own style of speech. Here are some practical tips for them to absorb and practice:

a. Stand up straight

b. Make good eye contact

c. Practice saying no to various imaginary scenarios

d. Say "No" to lesser requests friends and siblings make, like refusing to do the laundry for your brother or sister

e. Practice making no excuses for 'chores' others request. Just refuse without making up a reason for refusals

f. Avoid situations in which negative behaviors will be suggested by peers

g. Silently remind oneself of the negative results of the undesirable behavior

h. Walk away from the situation

i. Identifying peers who do not engage in negative or destructive behaviors and make friends with them

You as a parent no doubt have had experiences of others you knew when you were young who turned out very badly because they yielded to the pressures of engaging in self-destructive behaviors. For example, consider this story told by the father in this book:

22 Fairhaven Street

"I had a scholarship to go to college. Because the stipend for living expenses was very low, I had to settle for living in a rooming house. On the bottom floor, there was a young woman who went binge drinking a lot. One evening, when I came back from school, she was lying on the floor of the community kitchen there. Her ear lobe was bleeding because she tried to remove her earring while in a drunken stupor. She could barely walk and needed my assistance to go back to her room. A few months later, I heard that she was killed in a car crash. The others in the rooming house said he drove like a maniac when drunk.

On the second floor, lived the 'so-called' superintendent. He was supposed to clean the bathrooms and make minor repairs. Because he was always so high on drugs, he never took care of that. So, the community bathroom including the bathtub and sink was coated in green fungus. I tried to clean it myself, I puked when I tried. Besides, the fungus couldn't be removed. It was too thick. Whenever I wanted to shower, I did it in the public showers at the train station. They don't even have those anymore. That guy was getting paid by the slum landlord for doing nothing, and used all the money for drugs.

The alcoholic started drinking in junior high with a set of his 'drinking buddies'. The addicted guy was also lured into it by yielding to pressure from his 'friends'. Neither that alcoholic, nor the drug addict had any friends when I lived in that house.

Fortunately, I eventually rented a room at the house of an older woman who permit college kids to stay with her. I couldn't have parties or friends over, but that was a cheap price to pay, considering my options."

As you tell stories of your own, inform your teens that they may think they are the rare exceptions, and that they can resist overindulgence. Inform them that doesn't happen because of the nature of addiction. Certain biochemical "receptor" nerve cells are built up in one's brain, and create a craving for those substances. This is caused by an abnormal rise in the neurotransmitter, dopamine. As those cravings grow stronger, doses need to be larger in order to quell anxiety and obsession with obtaining the substances. Excessive dopamine can induce paranoia and psychotic-like behaviors.

4. Parents as Advisors

By the late preteen years and into the teenage years, it is most helpful to present choices to your children, rather than policing them. It gives them a sense of control, while you keep the doors open for dialogue. You are encroaching into the zone when penalties for bad behavior may only have limited success. Offer them your trust and your love. They can get a lot of steam from that to move into the right direction.

Reinforce their career goals, and provide opportunities for courses in the community that will give them a head start toward their chosen careers. Sometimes private mentors can be hired to give them a one-to-one exposure to their career choices. If they don't know what career they're interested in, you might assess their interests and skills that you've observed over the years, and encourage them to develop an interest related to those interests. Many colleges offer Liberal Arts degrees, but vocational schools teach specific skills that can help them make money immediately upon graduation. Most are just two-year schools, but they do have the option of attending college for two more years in order to get a Bachelor's degree.

5. Grades and Achievement

The father of the story here recalled a curious experience with his son, Brian. Brian, he recalled, was always extremely careful and rather geometric in his early drawings. He would get upset if he didn't have the right colors or strayed too far outside the lines. After taking a few tests and doing well, Brian became very cocky. He had a terrific memory, and began to feel that he "knew it all," and skimmed over his books. Amazingly, he continued to do well, although he wasn't at the top of his class. One day, he stomped into the door and complained.

"Mr. Huge didn't give me a good grade on my social studies paper."

"Mr. *Huge?*"

"That's what the kids call him. He is enormously fat!"

"Brian, don't give anyone a rude nickname, or point out a flaw you see in people. How do you think they would feel if they heard that sort of thing?"

"We don't call him 'Huge' or say he's fat in front of him."

"One of these days, Brian, you're going to slip. How would you feel if the kids called you by a rude name?"

"Sorry, Dad, but…"

"No 'but,' Brian."

"*OK, OK.* Well, anyway he talked about some of the kids' papers. He didn't say any names, but then he looked straight at me and said that he's not interested in hearing a lot of flowery terms and kibble to fill up space. He said he wanted to read papers with meat and substance... *Ha! Ha! 'Kibble' and 'Meat?'* Did you hear that? Food words!"

"Brian!" you said with a lower pitch to your voice. However, you had a silent grin about it in your mind. *He's going to be a clever and creative person someday,* you told yourself. Wit is a terrific psychological survival tool.

"Aw' right...I'll stop calling him 'Mr. Huge'," he said, trying to wipe the grin off his face. "His real name is 'Mr. Hughes'."

Mother was there, too, and she tittered a bit at the food words, stifling laughter. Emma, as usual, was eavesdropping and ran off giggling.

"And don't write that on the Internet, Emma!" Mom shouted.

Some teens just "sail" through high school because they are at least of average intelligence. They would rather just party with friends and forget there's any future for which they need to be prepared. They are intellectually lazy.

On the other hand, there are some who may or may not have a lot of cognitive abilities, but likewise are lazy. In order to avoid facing the fact that success depends upon achievement, and achievement requires hard work, they rationalize their laziness by developing the concept that is is not cool to be smart. They depend upon a system of social promotion by which school systems sometimes just pass them along. Occasionally, they'll attempt to send them to special schools or remediation education. Unless they are motivated, that too is unlikely to be successful. This is most tragic because these individuals become lost in life. They are high school dropouts. If they do manage to secure employment and maintain some acceptable level of job performance, they are deprived of the opportunity to get promotions which require high school diplomas. Vocational schools are good alternatives for them if – and only if – they develop the basic skills taught and are motivated to learn.

CONCLUSION

Although this is the end of the book, it is only the beginning for you. Reread it and develop some strategies of your own based on the real-life accounts. Study your children and determine if they are "Right-brained" (intuitive, creative) or "Left-brained" (logical, detail-oriented). Direct them toward careers in fields that feature one of the two elements. Of course, remember that even those given to logic may have an intuitive side of them which could be applied to creating or improving new products or even developing innovative ones. Inventors and entrepreneurs do that.

Help them learn to develop emotional intelligence. That is a lifelong task, but it helps to keep the engine of the higher mind in charge. It is invaluable in social interaction and employment.

Remember always that you are not a perfect parent. In all this world there is none. What matters are the hopes, the dreams, and the wonders of those whom you have raised. After you have weathered your way through raising your children...after you have cried, after you have laughed, after you have cared, and after you have tried; they will become all they can be – and even more – because of you.

Made in the USA
San Bernardino, CA
12 February 2018